The playing self is a groundbreaking new work from influ-ential cultural sociologist and clincial psychologist Alberto Melucci, best known for his writing on social movements and collective identities. In this book, based on and developing his *Il gioco dell'io* (1991), he delves deeper still into questions first addressed there about sub-jectivity, intimacy, and the self as both a psychological and socio-cultural entity, particularly in the context of global interdependence and planetary delimitations.

Alberto Melucci's phenomenological approach ac-counts for the self as a site of highly subjective and inti-mate experiences, such as crying, laughing and loving, and in relation to social structural dynamics, through more shared experiences, such as that of time, and links of the self to politics. In this way, he is able to explore the increasingly critical search for meaning at the boundary of visible collective processes and individual day-to-day experience, making a highly original connection between the two which draws on his own sociological and clinical practice.

D1127824

The playing self

Cambridge Cultural Social Studies

General editors: JEFFREY C. ALEXANDER, *Department of Sociology, University of California, Los Angeles, and* STEVEN SEIDMAN, *Department of Sociology, University at Albany, State University of New York.*

Editorial Board
JEAN COMAROFF, *Department of Anthropology, University of Chicago*
DONNA HARAWAY, *Department of the History of Consciousness, University of California, Santa Cruz*
MICHELE LAMONT, *Department of Sociology, Princeton University*
THOMAS LAQUEUR, *Department of History, University of California, Berkeley*

Cambridge Cultural Social Studies is a forum for the most original and thoughtful work in cultural social studies. This includes theoretical works focusing on conceptual strategies, empirical studies covering specific topics such as gender, sexuality, politics, economics, social movements, and crime, and studies that address broad themes such as the culture of modernity. While the perspectives of the individual studies will vary, they will all share the same innovative reach and scholarly quality.

Titles in the series
ILANA FRIEDRICH SILBER, *Virtuosity, charisma, and social order*
LINDA NICHOLSON AND STEVEN SEIDMAN (eds.), *Social postmodernism*
WILLIAM BOGARD, *The simulation of surveillance*
SUZANNE R. KIRSCHNER, *The religious and Romantic origins of psychoanalysis*
PAUL LICHTERMAN, *The search for political community*
KENNETH H. TUCKER, *French Revolutionary Syndicalism and the public sphere*

The playing self

Person and meaning in the planetary society

Alberto Melucci
University of Milan

CAMBRIDGE
UNIVERSITY PRESS

Published by the Press Syndicate of the University of Cambridge
The Pitt Building, Trumpington Street, Cambridge CB2 1RP
40 West 20th Street, New York, NY 10011-4211, USA
10 Stamford Road, Oakleigh, Melbourne 3166, Australia

First published 1996

Printed in Great Britain at the University Press, Cambridge

A catalogue record for this book is available from the British Library

Library of Congress cataloguing in publication data

Melucci, Alberto, 1943–
    The playing self: person and meaning in a planetary system /
Alberto Melucci.
        p.   cm. – (Cambridge cultural social studies)
    Includes bibliographical references.
    ISBN 0 521 56401 8. – ISBN 0 521 56482 4 (pbk.)
    1. Self.   2. Identity (Psychology).   3. Self – Social aspects.
4. Identity (Psychology) – Social aspects.   5. Social psychology.
6. Civilization, Modern – 20th century – Psychological aspects.
I. Title.   II. Series.
BF697.M453   1996
155.2–dc20   95-48270   CIP

ISBN 0 521 56401 8 hardback
ISBN 0 521 56482 4 paperback

Contents

Introduction

Each and every day we make ritual gestures, we move to the rhythm of external and personal cadences, we cultivate our memories, we plan for the future. And everyone else does likewise. Daily experiences are only fragments in the life of an individual, far removed from the collective events more visible to us, and distant from the great changes sweeping through our culture. Yet almost everything that is important for social life unfolds within this minute web of times, spaces, gestures, and relations. It is through this web that our sense of what we are doing is created, and in it lie dormant those energies that unleash sensational events.

This book deals with everyday life and tries to make sense of what individuals experience in it. A phenomenology of everyday experience is always as partial as the eye of the observer, but there can be no other point of departure for any investigation as to why, for us and so many others, things no longer 'add up': why is it that our routine gestures no longer are what they have been even in the recent past as we interact with different people, as we pass from one life ambit to another at work, at home, on holiday, or alone in solitude? And, above all, why is it so difficult to match the meaning of our behaviour with the words we use to name and recognize what we do?

We are trapped in a reality constructed by information – mostly, the particular kind of information that is constituted by images. Our existence, both in its routine and more dramatic moments, is created by information just as it depends on it. To feed ourselves we consume symbols, to love and reproduce we resort to the advice of experts, to desire and dream we use the language provided by the media. Even the threat of nuclear war, the very survival of our planet, hinges upon the control of information.

A society that uses information as its vital resource alters the constitutive structure of experience. The way we conceive reality and ourselves is changed in its cognitive, perceptive, and emotional dimensions: the representation of space and time, the relationship between possibility and reality, the link between natural phenomena and their symbolic elaboration are affected. Experience becomes an artificial construct: the product of relations and representations rather than of circumstances, the laws of nature, or contingency.

We lead our lives in the midst of a world of artefacts which no longer are mere *objects* but, instead, have become *processes of the mind*. We live by images, we clothe ourselves in messages, we make events happen by thinking them or by rendering them communicable. Yet this proliferation of material and symbolic artefacts does not cancel out what we naturally are: we have bodies and genes, we are part of an ecosystem, we stand between life and death. Daily life is scored by the marks of an unresolved tension between, on the one hand, the dynamic impulse to continuously create the new space and contents of experience, and, on the other hand, the need to observe the natural confines of experience itself. The ancient Taoist symbol of a jade ring expresses the relationship between fullness and emptiness, aptly conveying the tension between limit and possibility. The hole in the ring, the emptiness, introduces into the dense texture of the material the void – a space for a question that goes beyond what is visible, but yet a space which remains contained within the material itself. It is this tension that generates the questions about meaning that today go often unanswered.

We live on a planet that has become a global society, a society totally interconnected by its capacity of intervening on its environment and on social life itself, and yet still dependent on its natural home, the planet Earth. This twofold relation to the Earth, as the global field for social action and its physical boundary, defines the 'planetary society' in which personal life takes place. The accelerated pace of change, the multiplicity of roles assumed by the individual, the deluge of messages that wash over us expand our cognitive and affective experience to an extent that is unprecedented in human history. The points of reference used by individuals and groups in the past to plot their life courses are disappearing. Answering the basic question 'Who am I?' becomes progressively more difficult; we continue to need fixed anchor points in our lives but even our personal biographies begin to fail us as we hardly recognize ourselves in our memories. The search for a safe haven for the self becomes an increasingly critical undertaking, and the individual must build and continuously rebuild her/his 'home' in the face of the surging flux of events and relations.

I have traced this search in individual experience and contemporary collective phenomena, uncovering its dilemmas but also the potentialities contained in it. A world that lives by complexity and difference cannot escape uncertainty, and it demands from individuals the capacity to *change form* (the literal meaning of 'metamorphosis') while still continuing to be the same person. The constitutive dimensions of the self – time and space, health and sickness, sex and age, birth and death, reproduction and love – are no longer a datum but a problem. The self is no longer firmly pinned to a stable identity; it wavers, staggers, and may crumble. The term 'play' is also used as a mechanical term for the movement of a pivot pin that sits loosely in its housing, a free and unimpeded movement from or about a fixed point. The self, likewise, can succumb to trembling and lose itself, or it can learn to give itself 'play'.

To remain an individual self while learning how to change form emerges as an inevitable and central task confronting us today. The process of individuation must gain access to inner time, to those bodily and affective dimensions which enable us to see, feel, think, and communicate – that is, consciously to construct the field of our experience, playing ever new games. But if the self remains closed in on itself, unable to reach out to rise to the challenges of a planetary society pregnant with both potential and risk, the path of inner life may turn into an illusory flight from precisely such a responsibility or a silent prison of the self.

The problem is therefore how to preserve the relationship between fullness and emptiness symbolized by the jade ring: how to filter the teeming flow of messages that we emit and receive; how to find space for movement, but also for silence and stillness to grasp meanings that words can no longer convey. Without the ability to pass with fluency from one dimension to the other, from opening of the self to its closure, we shall be ultimately overwhelmed by the flow of information or swept aside from communication altogether.

Our day-to-day experience speaks to us of the presence of social changes that have a bearing more on the meaning of action than on the things themselves. In contemporary complex societies, the power built around social codification intervenes in the definition of the self and affects the biological and motivational structures of human action. At the same time, individuals gain wider control over the formation and orientation of their action. In proportion to the growth in the self-reflective capacity of individuals to produce information, communication, and sociality, complex societies face ever more urgently the necessity to intervene in that same action and on the ways it is perceived and represented by individuals and groups. In this manner, the two faces of change become apparent. On one side, the social and individual capacity to intervene in human action as it is produced increases; on the other, the generation of meaning is marked by the requirements of systemic control and regulation.

In this book, I want to venture into that frontier territory in which the more visible collective processes come into contact with individual experience and our day-to-day relations. A reflection on freedom that concerns itself with the meaning of individual existence and the destiny of the human species must make reference to both collective processes and subjective experience in everyday life. For this reason, I shall follow a circular route in my pursuit to bring out those areas of collective experience that today deeply affect individual life, at the same time tackling the collective import of those phenomena that on the surface may appear to be merely individual.

Moving around on the frontier territory calls for a special step. In the no-man's-land between well-known territories, knowledge becomes blurred and contaminated. This, however, is different from the confusion between already established languages. It is not necessary to know every word of the languages spoken on each side – and perhaps that would be even impossible. On the borders of the already familiar, one learns that 'elsewhere' the same thing is not quite the same; every time one returns with a slightly different point of view. At the frontier, one's vision of things is altered.

In this book I attempt to develop a viewpoint where we can better see what has gone largely unnoticed before our eyes. There is a naive way of looking that fails to achieve anything that reveals, simply reconnecting the signs of an already established universe to a reassuring confirmation of what was there from the beginning. But there exists another way of looking, one that enables us to *see*; a viewpoint that leads us beyond that which is taken for granted and allows us to reach towards what is invisible at first sight.

We have been accustomed to think that what matters is the aim and the outcome, that the means attain their importance subservient to the ends only. But the planetary changes through which we are now living call for a new kind of a perspective. If the road is made as important to us as its destination, the 'how' as significant as the 'what', then we shall be better able to hold both the jade ring and its hole, both the fullness and the emptiness. The 'how' can enrich the contents of experience with meaning, it can form the stable framework that allows us to let go what we have just lived when the moment is on hand for a passage to new contents. Without losing our selves, we can thus void our fullness and accept to change.

An understanding of what is currently happening to us can only emerge at the crossroads of various kinds of knowledge. In order to understand the modern self with its many faces we must alter our point of view, and adopt a way of seeing through which it becomes possible to grasp relational connections and learn from accumulated experience. It is becoming increasingly clear that human action is an interactive process, continuously constructed within a field of possibilities and limits. As a consequence of this realization, it becomes also evident that responsibility for our life on the planet Earth belongs to all of us. Social relationships and individual experience constitute thus the twin poles of the circular path that I wish to explore in this book.

In that, my approach will be phenomenological; the observer is not external to the field s/he describes, nor should s/he hesitate becoming passionately involved. Because my attention will be focused on the processes and not just the contents of experience, I shall concentrate on the frontiers where different territories of human action meet and merge with each other. It is these frontiers that I now invite the reader to explore.

As always in a no-man's-land, what one discovers has not yet developed its definite form and remains therefore ambivalent. The outcome of the processes I shall discuss in this book is thus entrusted to a freedom still to be constructed – a freedom that urges everyone to take responsibility for change.

A preliminary version of this book was first published in Italian in 1991. After *Nomads of the Present* (1989) where I had tried to connect social movements and individual needs in contemporary society, I wanted to devote a specific book to the results of my many years of research on the topic of individual experience in complex systems. At that time the boom of interest in the 'subjective' and cultural dimensions of social action was just beginning in the international sociological literature and the book could look like a lonely exploration by a sociologist with a penchant for psychology. Over the last few years the cultural trend toward 'subjectivity' has been confirmed resembling an explosion and a wide number of books have been published on these topics, including by influential authors and friends like Anthony Giddens, Zygmunt Bauman and Alain Touraine. This English book draws from its Italian older brother, but it has been completely rewritten as a new book which is intended to contribute to the current debates on the relationship between individual experience and societal changes.

In this book I present in a discoursive way ideas and findings assembled from a great deal of field research and during almost twenty years of clinical work in psychotherapy: some formal results were set out in a number of books written before this one, and many of the themes were also developed and got clarified in discussions with colleagues and students in various parts of the world. The classics of sociology, psychology and anthropology on which the book rests are rarely mentioned, no more than the philosophical background of my perspective: I have listed in a final bibliographical note only the more recent literature to which the reader can refer.

This book, together with its companion *Challenging Codes*, was first written with the linguistic assistance of Adrian Belton and at its intermediate stage I relied on the fundamental editing work of Timo Lyyra, whose invaluable help contributed substantially to improve both the form and the content of the text. Jeffrey Alexander, together with Steven Seidman, acted the way any author would dream of a series editor: he was supportive, generous and demanding. My editor at CUP, Catherine Max, was an understanding and reliable contact all along the publishing process, with a gentle touch that I could appreciate on many occasions. Let me thank them personally in Italian from the deep of my heart: *grazie*. Too many friends, colleagues and students discussed with me the ideas presented here, and by provoking a displacement of the point of view they contributed to the refinement or even the change of my perspective: Europe, the United States, Canada, East Asia, Latin America were the places where we met. I could not list all these voices by name, but I am deeply grateful to every one of them.

Milano, October 1995

1

The challenge of the everyday

Metaphors of time

We all have a spontaneous idea of what we mean when we talk about 'time'; the notion is immediate and intuitive. Yet when we try to define it, we have to resort to imagery, or perhaps to scientific language, which seems to serve as a kind of a *lingua franca* of today. Even when we understand immediately what we are talking about, we find it extremely hard to pin down what the experience of time actually means.

It is no coincidence that human beings have been puzzled about time since the dawn of history, and that they have conceived it as something so important and profound, something so constitutive of their experience, as to earn the status of the sacred. In more ancient cultures, reference to time always conjured up a divine image – often a river god or another aquatic deity which, in the image of the flow, reflects the appearance and disappearance of things and encloses the cosmos in the circular movement depicted by another traditional symbol, the serpent biting its tail. Fluid and enfolding, the experience of time is characterized by a sense of thickness and a density that our definitions seldom provide and which, perhaps for this reason, cultures have sought to convey through the means of metaphor and myth.

This perhaps explains why the experience of time is so diversified. While the West has conceived time as a category having to do with the present, the past, and the future, many aboriginal cultures do not distinguish between inner and outer events, rather associating different times with different experiences. The Hopi people of the Southwest United States, for instance, make the distinction between the time which is (as the time of objects) and the time of whatever is about to come about (the time of subjective experiences, feelings and emotions). Time, for them, is a multiplicity of events, with each event characterized by a specific temporal dimension of its own.

The various forms of time conceived thus flow all in different directions. There is an extraordinary similarity in conceptualization between this kind of idea of time and the one described by genetic psychology as typifying the experience of young children. In early childhood, our temporal categories are in fact constituted by dimensions of locality. For a child, every action and every experience is connected to its own particular time instead of a constant uniform flow of events as a single temporal sequence.

Among the many symbolic representations that historical cultures have created for the inexpressible dimension of time, three recurrent figures emerge. The first is that of the *circle*. Time is perceived and lived as the cyclical renewal of all things, unfolding according to a law laid down by a primordial and atemporal event which repeats itself in visible events governing their regular appearance and disappearance. Thus, for example, the mythical time of the tribe's founding moment, or the sacred time of a culture's fundamental experiences, returns cyclically in events which perpetuate it and at the same time celebrate it. Things repeat themselves, and, as in the great cycles of nature inspiring the image of the circle, nothing is ever definitively acquired or lost. We can find the circle symbol employed in cultures very distant from each other in space and time, from the ancient Chinese cultures to those of the Native Americans and medieval Europeans, and altogether it reflects the special relationship between all traditional cultures and the deep-seated rhythms of nature.

The modern age – that is, the West arisen on the foundation of technical rationality – has imposed another pattern on the experience of time; it descends to us from the Judaeo-Christian tradition. While preserving the basically cyclical image of time, Christianity introduced an additional notion to it: the genesis and the end of the world as marking the limits of a linear progression. The history of the world came to be seen as a depiction of man's downfall and redemption – as the story of his salvation, whose most profound meaning would be revealed only at the journey's end. The modern age inherited this idea, divested it of its religious garb, and expressed it in terms of progress, of the wealth of nations, of revolution, of time which flowed towards its own extinction, towards a timeless standstill for which all previous stages are only a preparation. The circle symbol was thus replaced by the *arrow*: time began somewhere, and it had an end that also served as its culmination – a final point which defined the meaning of the entire trajectory and illuminated its intermediate stages.

This was also the idea that propelled industrialization and brought about the great transformation of the Western world that resulted in the consolidation of the form which the entire planet now accepts – or endures. Whether couched in terms of decline or of progress, the linear pattern of the arrow has penetrated to the deep roots of Western culture and still today profoundly shapes our conception of time. We remain looking forward to a salvation which, to be sure, may of course no longer be religious: to a secularized salvation entrusted to the powers of techno-scientific rationality, to development, to economic growth – in every case something which projects the meaning of the present into the future.

However, even the figure of the arrow by which we seek to capture our experience of time, the image of a purposive sequence, is now losing its hold. We see around us the great myths of modernity fading away, the narratives which promised ultimate salvation dissolving. Our experience of time undergoes increasing fragmentation as our future grows more uncertain and perhaps more ominous than ever before: what looms in the horizon is today catastrophe. We no longer possess the certainty of a radiant future and final salvation as the destiny of history. Linear time yields to an experience of transitions without development, to a movement between disconnected points, a sequence of fleeting moments whose meaning is entirely grounded in the present point of time. It is precisely this experience, our perception of time as a discontinuous and point-like sequence, which has given rise to a new figure: the motif of the *point*.

Measuring and perceiving

The cycle, the arrow, and the point are then the metaphors with which the different human cultures have set to define time. But more than being mere cosmographic vocabulary, these organizing concepts convey different ways of living in the time. The diversity of cultures and the diversity of individuals refer us back to the great divide between experiencing and naming which I introduced in the beginning. Yet, in spite of this variety of perceptions and images, men have always tried to measure time. As cultures have sought to circumscribe the fluid, aquatic divinity which swamps everything and gushes in all directions, they have in one way or another confined it using measurements so as to build firm embankments with which at least to give direction to its flow. Cultures, that is to say, have invented ways to measure the immeasurable.

The ways in which time is measured tell us a great deal about how it is experienced. Here, too, the modern age has made a decisive break with the past. The time which we all have inherited from modernity is the time measured by clocks. It is the time which sets the cadence of our daily routines, organizes social life, assigns positions, gauges the gaps between them, decides the value of work. Clocks are machines, instruments which measure time as if it were a homogeneous and divisible quantity. They thus both presuppose and create the standardization of time. Clock time is equal unto itself, divisible into smaller units, and the same wherever and however it is experienced.

The cultures of the past measured times in the most disparate ways, but all of them were directly or indirectly connected with the four elements of earth, fire, wind, and water. The measuring of time has always been guided by the idea of flux already discussed, and its instruments have always represented attempts to capture, contain, and freeze that flux. Pre-modern cultures invented devices which used water, sand, wind, a slowly burning flame, or sunlight to measure time. They searched for time in the intrinsic motion of the elements, as if the mere fact of giving a material or visible form to its eternal flux could circumscribe it.

Observing a slowly burning candle or the running sand in an hour-glass is a perceptive and spatial experience; duration is filled with sensory referents, and a relationship is established with the material element. A clock transforms time into an abstract trajectory through space, although its moving hands still maintain a physical relationship between visual perception and the measurement of time. In the mechanical abstraction and standardization of duration that the clock performs, however, there still persists a constant reference to sequence and to flux, made visible by the relationship among the various points on the dial. When we say, 'It's five minutes before ...' or 'It's ten minutes after ...' we are using a perceptual measurement of time which still involves a physical relationship with space, be it no more than the small circuit traversed by the hands of the clock.

The invention of the digital clock, however, has eliminated this last extant reference to space and introduced a new measurement of time: an entirely cognitive pulsation which at any moment of time turns continuum into a series of dots. Time thus becomes merely the reading of signs and their abstract mental processing. The gaze that followed the movement of sand, of a flame, of a wheel or a shadow established a relationship with the 'material', with the sign it expressed, and with the symbolic dimension in which that particular measurement of time was meaningful. The circular movement of the hands of a mechanical clock still preserves a trace of this original relationship. It is given material form and continues to incorporate the memory of the cycle. The arrow is already present and paramount, but the circle has not yet disappeared from the perceptive horizon and is therefore still meaningful.

But when the measurement of time becomes purely a matter of reading of numbers, an uninterrupted but discontinuous sequence of signs, an electronic vibration of immutable regularity, then the point becomes paramount, and our experience of duration, of continuity, of the relationship between 'before' and 'after' is profoundly changed. The question of whether it is the clocks that create time, or whether it is time that creates the instruments for its measurement, is otiose. The representation of time and its measurement are two aspects of the same problem: namely, giving meaning to experience. Thus the purpose behind my reference to clocks has been to show how profoundly the way we 'live' time has changed. Clock time is divisible into wholly equal units, while the measurements used before the invention of the clock allowed for more labile and diffuse subdivisions. The fact that today we can answer the question, 'How much time do we have left?' by resorting to a combination of digits gives a univocality and precision to our perception of time which no previous 'natural' measurement could achieve. And upon the disappearance of the last trace of the natural heritage of the movement of the clock hand through the cycle of hours, the answer has become encoded in a sign which we can only passively register.

Times of experience

Time measured by the clock, wrote Fernando Pessoa, is false because it is divided spatially, from the outside. We may not agree with the wholesale rejection of the significance of clock measurement as simply false, but it certainly differs from subjective experience. Our experience of time rarely if ever coincides with what the clock tells us. Long before Pessoa, Augustine had concluded that time belongs to the soul and inquired whether it was possible to connect the diverse moments of time in subjective experience. Today, the relation between past, present, and future constitutes a question that addresses the very roots of our individuality.

This relation may be represented most simply as linear. The past contains what has been, thus preparing for the present, which in turn acts as a prelude to what is yet to come: the future. Something therefore exists which disappears from presentness, something which is present, and something which as yet is not part of presentness but will eventually be. This linear relation, however, is anything but simple, since we live in both that linearity and other, multi-dimensional patterns of time at the same time. For example, the future is shaped by the conditions and constraints of our past. The odds are never entirely wide open: the past charts the confines of the possible and the future is born bearing its imprint. What is really to come, as Heidegger stated, is what has actually been. Thus the future is already contained in the past and bred by the past – at least in the sense that what we have been can never wholly be erased by the new ways we might take, and even when we take new ways, we shall never have an entirely limitless array of possibilities laid out before us.

There is, however, another side to this relation, creating an apparent paradox which the experience of time cannot escape. While we remain aware that the future is born of the past, it is equally true that the past is also continuously shaped by the future. Whenever we confront the possible – as in planning for the future – when we make a decision that anticipates the action to come, the past is re-examined, amended, and given a new meaning. We thus continually rewrite our own pasts and that of the world. Our memory is selective and reconstructs history and biography according to a project for the future.

Hence, the linear relation is flanked by a circular one. Our tomorrow is conditioned by the matrix of the past, but our present experience continuously reads and elaborates what we have been, in new ways that prepare the future. This bond between past and future can only be forged in the realm of the present: presentness is the place where past and future meet in a circular relationship. It is within the present that the past throws its light and shadow onto the future, illuminating or obscuring that part of us in which we wish, or are actually able, to recognize ourselves.

The line – which is more tied to the 'objectivity' of external events and closer to clock time – is thereby matched by the circle, which principally conveys our inner relationship with ourselves, with our bodies, and with our biographies. When we talk about our lives we cannot escape the circle that joins memory and the project together. But even more importantly, it is precisely in the point of the present that this link is formed. Whenever we feel that we can consciously, decisively, and purposively project ourselves towards the future because we can rely on what we have been, or whenever the fire of the project throws new light on the events and relations of memory, we know that the point-like moment of the present condenses the fullness of our experience. But we also know that the flux will be interrupted if we prove unable to tie the threads of the past and the future together in the 'now-time' in which we are immersed; the present is then already lost to our need to retain and our anxiety to anticipate.

We thus live all the patterns of time simultaneously: the recurring circle of memory and project, the linear projection of the arrow as an intention and a goal, the exalted condensation of the point, or the experience of losing ourselves in disconnected fragments. It is often difficult to reconcile these patterns, since each one of them brings us to the borders of the others. The repetition of the cycle follows the trajectory of hopes but also of disappointments; the linear progress towards an end goal enthuses us but also saps our energy as we wait; the point escapes us whenever we try to hold on to it.

The wisdom of the past contained a pattern which we can see synthesizing these contradictory experiences. The magical and initiationary sign of the spiral unites the cycle, the arrow, and the dot in a single movement which constantly turns back onto itself, but every time on a different plane. Through the ages, the idea of the spiral has been known to different cultures from the Mesopotamian empires to medieval alchemy. The spiral tells us that the circle and the arrow can be united in their rotation around the point: circular movement and forward thrust are bound together by a common need to find a central anchor. The pattern of the spiral fascinates us because it is a challenge to the dilemmas of time, an attempt to give shape to the deep-seated desire that animates us whenever we encounter the plurality of dimensions and movements that constitutes our temporal experience. The circular movement that advances in space expresses the all-too-human dream of a flux that is also in a standstill.

As the spiral returns to itself on always different planes, it signals another fundamental dimension of temporal experience: the rhythm. We are natural beings within an ecosystem, and our biological lives are profoundly conditioned by the rhythms of day and night, the cycles of the moon and of the seasons, the circadian rhythms that mark the day-by-day cadences of our bodily functions, the vital rhythmic pulsations of our breathing and heartbeat which keep us alive. These rhythms of nature give manifest physical form to the pattern of the spiral, since they comprise circularity but also metamorphosis, cyclical regularity but also change and flux. Our time is not solely the time of the clock, but nor is it merely that of the soul: it is also the time which brings flowers into bloom, which regulates the great animal migrations, and which triggers the metamorphosis that gives birth to a butterfly. It is within these rhythms of nature weaving human time together that repetition and change are conjoined.

Rhythmicity also brings with it the alternation of speed and slowness, of movement and stillness. As one season succeeds another with the rhythm of breathing, nature's time alternates tension with distension, acceleration with pause, accumulation with emission. We may forget such time imprinted in our bodies but we cannot exist without it. We can respect it or we can violate it, but our temporal experience, whether we recognize it or not, is also the great breath that joins us with the cosmos.

Constructing time and space

Industrial capitalism, the societal model that formed us, has left us with a figure of time in which two images predominate: the machine and the goal. The time of modern society is measured by machines which create an artificial and objective definition of temporal experience. The time of the mechanical clock is not marked by the cycles of day and night, of the seasons, of birth and death, and it is no longer tied to human perception. The time measured by machines is a universal standard which enables the comparison and exchange of values, performances, and rewards. It is a homogeneous quantity. As the equivalent of money, it is in itself a quality-neutral intermediary which enters all the calculations on which instru-mental rationality is founded. In the organization of work and in company balance sheets, in everyday life and in the public calendar, mechanical time makes no distinction between individual experience and the rhythm of society; everything can be measured, divided, and calculated using the stan-dard yardstick of quantity.

The second characteristic of the modern conception of time is its end-directed orientation to which I already referred at the beginning of this chapter. Time has a definite direction, the meaning of which is acquired by the final goal. The emphasis placed by industrial culture on the central role of history presupposes through its myths of progress and of revolution that time is articulated in relation to an end: all the intermediate stages are illu-minated by a beacon at the end of the path which invests the actions per-formed along the way with meaning. Work ethic, militancy, accumulation, saving – these are all patterns of behaviour typical of industrial culture. They are all oriented towards a goal and based on the idea that the time will eventually come when everything so laboriously striven for will be finally acquired and enjoyed.

Today, when the various times of our everyday existence differ so much from each other as to be mutually antithetical, this model nevertheless strikes us as alien. There are now measurable times and times which are impossible to measure; there are diluted times and vastly accelerated times. The images of television, graphics, and advertising introduce a multiplicity of times into everyday life, they shuttle us instantly from the past to the future and back again. They constantly switch us between one temporal rhythm and another. There are blanks, gaps, and interruptions in the movement between such different times, fragmenting our perception of continuity and demanding a capacity for rapid shifts, frequent adjustments, and flexibility, as well as a capability to synchronize.

The sharpest of these divisions are those between interior times – the times of desire and of dreaming, of the affections and the emotions – and outer times – today increasingly measured by social rules and without the homogeneity they possessed in the past. The clear divide between inner times and social times is nothing new in the history of cultures; in the past, however, the relative smoothness and slowness of change ensured a certain integration between the subjective temporal experience and the time that was socially defined and regulated. In today's highly differentiated systems, people act through multiple social memberships and occupy diverse roles as family members, workers, citizens, consumers and so forth. Temporal rules are almost always specific to each of these various domains, and we are thus constantly obliged to pass from one reference system to another, and from these again onward to the more intimate dimensions of experience.

Coping with these gaps, voids, and dissonances becomes increasingly difficult; in fact, from this derives the underlying cause of a number of new pathologies which I will examine below. Such pathologies, however, represent only the extreme form of the responses and behaviors which have now become characteristic of everyday life. One of these widespread manifestations is the tendency to extend the subjective dimensions of time by resorting to artificial forms of sensory stimulation so as to produce altered states of consciousness. The use of chemical stimulants, over-exposure to noise and visual stimulation, and a surrender to rhythmic and repetitive movement are all ways to expand inner time. They express, in a paradoxical fashion, an attempt to recompose the inner world and to reassemble the fragments of temporal experience into a unity of some kind. The borderline between the discovery and the loss of the self becomes thereby very blurred, and what is actually produced is more commonly a sort of desensitization – an anaesthesia caused by excess of stimulation which annihilates all interior space. Drugs, music, and dancing had an important place in traditional societies, but in them they were an integral part of a ritual order which assigned them a function in social life and in the individual's inner life-course. The breaking with everyday order that ritual permitted and made possible expanded subjective time and gave access to new dimensions of the self. However, this escape from the dominance of routine was itself part of a sacred order which confirmed that same rule and helped to recover the bond between the individual and the community.

In contemporary societies the extreme gesture of drug abuse is a dramatic signal and the most manifest symptom of an almost unbridgeable split between inner and outer times. On a less dramatic scale, other symptoms abound which testify to the search for artificial release from the pressures of social time; among these we could count examples ranging from exotic tourism to cathartic bodily experiences and the totalitarian paradises of neo-mystical sects. The ambivalence of these phenomena cannot be ignored: they readily lend themselves to manipulation and loss of individual freedom, but they are also an unmistakeable sign of the unresolved tension between the manifold of times that modulates the cadence of everyday life. The differentiation of time has brought along with it new problems. I have already mentioned the difficulty of relating such divergent times to one standard measurement. Yet there is still the need to integrate them all into a collective framework of shared social rules and within a personal biography in order for the actor to be able to constitute her/himself in unity and continuity.

A differentiated time, moreover, is a time without history, or rather a time in which numerous independent histories unfold simultaneously. Hence it is a time which is not directed towards a final outcome: a time which assigns an inestimable value to the present because nothing of what has been will return, and nothing of what is will be redeemed in the end. This, however, gives rise to a paradoxical condition, since it is impossible for human beings not to remember and project themselves towards the future. A livable human life without memory and project would be inconceivable. But the problem that arises here is precisely how to anchor the breathing of time into the present, how to divest ourselves of the past without forgetting it, and how to anticipate what is to come without being consumed in the wait.

Lastly, multiple and discontinuous time explicitly reveals its nature as a cultural artefact that is entirely constructed within everyday social relationships. The industrial organization of work had already dissolved the natural cycle of day and night. Today, all the times of nature are subject to social intervention which modifies them when it does not completely annihilate them. The seasonal cycles have disappeared from our dining tables now that so much of our food has lost every relation to the natural time of harvest. Holiday brochures promise us tropical sun or winter snow all year round, feeding to the illusion that we can ignore the cycle of the seasons. Even birth and death, the paramount events of natural time, have lost their inevitability and become products of medical and social intervention, as we shall see in chapter 6.

In reality, however, it is not only time that has become a construct; the other fundamental category that governs our experience, our representation of space, has been profoundly altered as well. The physical space to which we have traditionally referred was a measurable reality, and we perceived it according to preestablished dimensions, learning through experiences and comparisons how to assess it. This manner of defining space is now challenged by new phenomena which have radically affected our habitual spatial referents. In this respect, too, we find ourselves in a paradoxical situation in which the unrestricted expansion of an abstract space accessible through advances in information services and communications proceeds simultaneously with its seemingly unlimited compression, along with the recent developments of miniaturization technologies. In both cases, any relationship to the physical space of ordinary human experience has lost its meaning.

Information, the central resource of our society, disrupts spatial relationships – above all the relationship between space and its dimensions. The past societies based on the accumulation of material goods always took space to be a physical resource as all things were bound to their perceptible dimensions. Regardless of whether men, money, or machines were accumulated, space had to be created to accommodate them, and spatial dimensions were necessary to transfer or to exchange them. Information, however, can be contained in an infinitesimal point. Over the last twenty years, the accelerated speed of evolution of information technologies has abolished every correspondence between the quantity of information and the space required to store it. Enormous masses of data can be gathered in a fraction of a second and in a minimal space, and their transfer or exchange is no longer directly conditioned by the physical dimensions of the objects concerned or by spatial distances.

Information technology has transformed also another fundamental spatial relationship, that of proximity and distance. Images bring us constantly into contact with spaces alien to our direct physical experience. Planetary space is by now a routine datum of our daily lives, and we increasingly relate to spaces that extend even beyond our planet. With the massive reduction in the time required to transit great distances, and with the accessibility of practically every point on the globe, the symbolic expansion and the perceptual contraction of space are further reinforced.

The concepts of large and small, near and far, thereby cease to relate solely to measurable quantities. They are now symbolic indicators, cultural artefacts organizing a space which is no less real than the physical space. As a system of spatial reference, geography of the landscape has therewith given way to a geography of the mind. Together with time, space becomes multiple and discontinuous and we are compelled to change our yardsticks, to combine quantity and quality, to position ourselves, and to move with great flexibility.

Nevertheless, we still inhabit a physical space, we still handle objects endowed with physical dimensions, we still have to cover distances physically. Here, too, new problems arise. Multidimensional experience devoid of fixed spatial referents creates bewilderment and rootlessness, and movement through space becomes an end in itself. We are constantly on the move, we travel much more than we ever used to, we visit other countries; but we often do so aimlessly and unaware of where we really are.

As we are getting used to inhabiting a space lived principally on the symbolic plane, the relationship with our bodies tends to be sundered. The body thus loses its spatial skills and its ability to test its own limits. We must then resort to physical exercise and to hobbies to relearn the elementary skills required to move in physical space, to measure distances in terms of our own physiques, to handle objects. The children of the great metropolises, living through images and journeying by symbols, have to enrol in specialized programmes or take extra-curricular courses to make it possible for them to learn anew the simple art of inhabiting a body in space.

The experience of space as a multi-dimensional and open artefact is in danger of turning into its opposite. Where every experience of space becomes interchangeable, our world may merge into an unrelieved monotone, equal in all its dimensions and always the same – like the small towns of the American Mid-west whose only distinguishing feature is the variable placement of their McDonald's and Coca Cola signs. Today we may move as we please, but we know nothing of the land we are travelling through. Basically, we do not even really care: like tourists on exotic vacation packages we could equally be in Australia, the Caribbean, or Acapulco.

Inner rhythms, social rhythms, rhythms of the cosmos

As already noted, social time in the modern world is linear. It is distinguished by the continuity and uniqueness of events which succeed each other in one and only one direction and are therefore irreversible. Hence, it is possible to talk of a 'before' and an 'after', and one can also establish a cause-effect relationship between what precedes and what follows: there are always previous events which determine the subsequent ones. Social time is measurable and predictable, because its different segments can be compared and because the past renders the future in a distinct sense calculable. Finally, social time is uniform: for every event there is an established cadence, a fixed rhythm on which we base our expectations and on whose maintenance the social order depends.

Inner time, the time which is associated with affections and emotions and inhabits the body, has quite different features. It is multiple and discontinuous; in it, different times coexist, succeed one another, intersect, and overlap in subjective experience. There is a cyclical time in which, like in mythical time, events return largely as they were before and manifest themselves in the body, in the emotions, and in dreams, symptoms, images, and repetitive patterns of behaviour.

Then, there is simultaneous time: many times exist contemporaneously – yesterday and tomorrow, my time and yours, here and elsewhere. We can be adults and children, black and white, beforehand and afterwards. The simultaneity of inner time ignores the law of noncontradiction.

Hence, time is also multidirectional: events can be correlated by moving forwards or moving backwards, by switching to alternative times or by remaining within simultaneity. Inner time is thus constantly reversible: what happens today can alter our past; an event which affects a loved one may upset the way we judge the future; nothing is ever given once and for all.

In inner experience time is not measurable. Our perceptions of duration vary according to the moment and the situation; indeed, on certain occasions time may cease to flow and come to a standstill. There are discontinuities and breaks which may obstruct its continuous movement. Inner rhythms vary; they never belong entirely to just one category of experience; there are moments of anguish or reflection which take an eternity to pass while entire days can slip by in an instant.

The opposition between inner time and social time therefore could not be more pronounced. Culture has the function of reducing the pressure of this noncongruence by availing means by which inner time can be symbolically expressed, as through art, play, myths, and sacred rituals. But there also exist domains of individual experience where the two times can coexist: sleep, imagination, love. However, the contradiction between the two develops again whenever inner personal times clash with the requirements of social regulation in a more direct fashion. This is what happens, for example, in the relationship between adult and the child, in the treatment of insanity, and in the social definition of deviance. In personal life it is illness which reveals the incompatibility between inner time and social time. The illness of the body serves as an expression of a word which cannot otherwise be uttered, and the mute voice of the symptom signals the need for inner reality to be heard.

A flexible transition from one of these planes to another seems today to be one of the most important conditions for personal equilibrium, and it forms a crucial point where new difficulties and sufferings typical of our time arise. These difficulties are an organic part of the experience of living in a world of rapid change; a world in which the range of opportunities open to us is infinitely wider than what our capacity for action can effectively handle. The experience that we have acquired and committed to memory shrinks, for change rushes on in its course and compels us to incessantly reinterpret the past in the light of the data accumulated in the present. At the same time, the future weighs upon us and continually obliges us to make choices, predictions, and decisions.

The surfeit of possibilities available to us far exceeds what we can effectively cope with and utilize, and our everyday life is choked with opportunities which we are unable to seize. One need only leaf through a holiday brochure or a catalogue selling merchandise like computers and television sets, with all their options, to feel a mixture of attraction and impotence. Even if we were able to afford it, we could never go simultaneously to the Maldives and the Seychelles, to Florida and the South of France. Likewise we could never watch all the ninety-nine channels on our television set at the same time – even learning all the features available in our home computer requires far more time than we can actually ever invest in utilizing them. Our freedom of choice and the plethora of opportunities availed to us tell us that time is short, that we must always leave something behind; it is this dilemma that frequently lies at the sources of the fundamental experience of frustration.

Insufficient time, the necessity to choose, and the renunciation of many possibilities that any action entails seem to generate many of the central difficulties and hardships experienced in everyday life. Complexity creates pressures in people's lives, to which they respond by attempting to adjust. Efforts are often frustrated, and the failure provokes suffering, sometimes pathologies. A first response to complexity consists in disowning the future. There are too many opportunities, change is too rapid; personal limitations, social constraints, and our previous histories prevent us from grasping and keeping to what we desire. We give up and allow the past to overflow into the present and engulf it, thereby yielding to resignation before the future. Depression is the state when we are submerged by the past and we relinquish our hold on the future because we cannot cope with its rhythm and its scope. The past is our anchor, a safe haven which turns into a prison.

At the opposite extreme stands another response: disowning the past. If there are so many opportunities, if things change so rapidly, then we must pursue everything, consume everything as fast as we can and forgo nothing. A kind of Don Giovanni syndrome impels us to chase after every opportunity, only to then swiftly abandon each one of them in favour of another one beckoning next to it. The tension induced in the process produces stress symptoms, as the body's response to the lack of time and to our fear that we may have missed our chance. In its most severe form, stress may precipitate a breakdown of the self, and ultimately schizophrenia. When the attempt to hold all the possibilities together fails, one can at least try to organize their apartness by creating a deceptive autonomous totality out of each separate fragment of the self.

A third type of response is to disown the present. Such a reaction seems to take on two principal forms. The first consists of filling the present with the future. When we are entirely absorbed by the project, by what is still to come, anxiety takes over the present and we are effectively immobilized. Alternatively, fearing that we may miss one of the opportunities open to us, we deny all of them their meaning to blunt their appeal. The present becomes bereft of content; it is now motionless and we deliberately stop short of getting involved in any possible choice. We are bored – 'boredom' being those thoughts without thought, those desires without desire that adorn our immobility.

A final response to the shortage of time is associated with the dimension of rhythm and the alternation of speed and slowness, action and repose. Either consumed by the fire of an exhausting pace, or benumbed by slowness that we feel with a sense of guilt, we are unable to live the alternation, we remain prisoner to one pattern or the other, never finding the rhythmic pulse that connects movement and stasis.

These responses show that the pressures of social time are mainly physical in their effect. Anxiety, suffering, and even illness are a testimony to the hard labour of living in time, a time imposed on us by our culture but also shaped by our conscious choices. Our attachment to a past which overwhelms present and future, our futile attempts to pursue all possibilities, the way we fill the present with anxiety or freeze it in boredom so that it acquires a degree of permanence, and, lastly, the difficulty in finding a rhythm as the alternation of speed and slowness, action and repose – these are all manifest signals speaking of the difficulties involved in adapting to the age of complexity.

Today, temporal experience is a multiple and discontinuous process which combines all the dimensions examined in this chapter. It is the cement that binds the past, present, and future, and fuses memory and project in the here and now. It weaves the line and the circle together, and at times draws us into the spiral at the moments of grace when we find ourselves back at the same point but on a different plane. Our experience of time is constituted by speed and slowness, by movement and repose: by alternation and rhythm. Our experience is both reversible and irreversible, for we stand on the line that leads from birth to growth, to old age, to death; but we also live within a time that can return to retrace the cycle, as in our inner experiences – for no less it is the time of the soul, of which Augustine reminds us.

Today it is a problem of recognizing this plurality. We must not consent to the reduction of our experience of time to only one of its dimensions. Our quest for unity places us in daily confrontation with the reality of the increasing contradiction between clock/calendar time and inner times – a contradiction which constantly challenges us to find a linkage or a continuity between the various realms of experience. We cannot be everywhere, we cannot be everything, we often end up living only in a succession of discrete moments. A point-like time may well amount to fragmentation of time, to the dissolution of the legacy bequeathed to us from the cultures of the past. But the point-like dimension no less contains riches in itself: through it is created a chance to reactivate the realm of presentness through living moment by moment, weaving together the fabric of continuity. The unity of time is no longer guaranteed by our roots in the past and our memories, nor by the projects for the future; it is secured only by our capacity to be present in the now-time. The challenge of the present is therefore to construct an experience of time which may enable us to pass through variety and multiplicity without losing our selves in the process.

Achieving an equilibrium of the rhythms of nature can thus only be the outcome of a surplus of awareness. It can never be produced regressively by an ingenuous belief in a Mother Nature endowed with magical powers and a will to teach us her laws. Nature, too, is a culturally interpreted reality, a reality in which we intervene ever more directly. To bring nature into existence and to encounter it with respect would mean today that our field of experience be expanded to include awareness of our biological rhythms and the fundamental cycles within and without us. These rhythms, however, will not operate as the 'pure', natural forces they once were: they may still turn against us if ignored or violated, but they will become part of our everyday experience of time to the extent that we are able to consciously accept their presence.

Such is then the difference between our culture and all those of the past. We now possess the power to intervene in nature, including our own inner nature. As a consequence, natural time no longer exists; and it is useless to cultivate the illusion that it would still be possible to recreate a pure nature which can deliver us from the necessary evils of civilization. This fact notwithstanding, there still exists a natural time which can be culturally safeguarded by awareness of it and by responsibility for it. The paradox and the challenge is that we may, culturally, become nature. This, moreover, is in fact our only chance in a world which by now is almost completely constructed by ourselves – a world whose natural dimension we can either bring into existence or destroy.

However, this is not to imply that we are no longer factually born, that we no longer fall ill, that we no longer die; nor is it to say that we are exempt from the extremely delicate constraints of the ecosystem that surrounds us. But the difference between us and the cultures of the past is that these restrictions can become the object of cultural awareness and be culturally elaborated – for we intervene in nature using the power of knowledge, technology, and our decisions, and this includes the nature which constitutes us as a species. Other cultures have simply recognized and accepted such constraints as imposed on them by the authority of a higher being or order. In any case, this difference does not release us from these constraints, but it does provide us with the possibility to choose them consciously and at will. No other culture of the past has possessed the ability to decide on its own limits in a comparable manner for the simple reason alone that no previous society has developed a capacity to destroy itself. No society of the past generated a power over itself that would have enabled it to envisage its own self-destruction.

All this means that it is now a matter of our own decision whether we are to survive or suffer a catastrophe, whether we are willing to accept, reject, or overcome our limitations. It is not enough to throw ourselves upon the whims of nature; we have to choose and 'create' nature (starting from respect for it) through a productive expansion of culture and of awareness, through our capacity for presentness which begins in everyday space and time.

2

Needs, identity, normality

The needing self

The perception that we are lacking something seems to be one of the main-springs of our behaviour. The human species ceased to belong entirely to nature as only one animal species among many when, through developed language, it learned to give a symbolic representation to such a perception of lack and absence and the accompanying urge to overcome it. A culture is a symbolic universe which contains the gestures, the actions, and the words with which the fundamental experience of absence – as limit, death, and otherness – can be expressed.

Of this expressive ability were born meaningful action, the capacity to produce (harnessing forces of nature to overcome the constraints imposed by nature and to transform it), and the will to reproduce culturally. When children no longer represent just the biological perpetuation of the species but, instead, are invested with affections, expectations, and tasks intended to ensure the survival of the group, reproduction becomes culture. Hunger ceases to be a biological need when the gathering and the preparing of food is given a name, organized by group relations and regulated by codes. Even our basic physiological functions respond to a cultural code which decides what is clean and what is dirty, what is pure and what is impure.

If, then, there is no biological need that has not already been organized by language and social relations, it is impossible to talk of needs exclusively in natural terms. Every human need is an interpersonal and therefore social construct which uses language to express the perceived lack and the urge to overcome it.

In our everyday lives, common sense tends to treat needs as natural and immediate phenomena to which a person responds spontaneously. Although the process of responding to needs appears to be wholly sub-jective, it nevertheless involves a cultural construction which extends even to the most trivial of acts. We always move within a shared domain of language. Whenever we name a feeling, whenever we utter a need, we establish a bridge between deep, subjective, primarily sensory experience, on the one hand, and the network of social relations to which we belong and from which we draw the words to describe our experiences, on the other.

For example, if we are thirsty – if, that is, we feel the physiological stimulus to drink – and respond by drinking water rather than fruit juice, we are operating within a culturally organized field which enables us to give linguistic expression to our needs and to satisfy them within an already constructed social frame of reference. As inhabitants of a socially constructed reality, our capacity to elaborate needs in cultural terms has reached a point where even our most commonplace wants are directed towards objects with a highly symbolic connotation. We no longer simply feel thirsty, hungry, or unclothed; our feelings of lack have already been oriented towards specific objects that are constructed symbolically by information, the market, advertising, and the social networks to which we belong. So we are thirsty for A, we can only wear B, for breakfast we want C; and hence we actually define our needs within the specific codes of the everyday cultural field in which we live and communicate.

While, to be sure, the definition of needs has always been culturally produced, it is today more evident than before that needs are the result of social construction. At the same time, however, we are witnessing a paradoxical call for a return to the natural roots of needs. We have already begun to intervene in the biological structure of our species and to probe the delicate borderline between mind and body – a polarity which the language that we use to talk about our experience of lack, by separating needs from desires, also expresses.

On the one hand, we refer to needs as if they were natural. There is a tendency in scientific research, for example, to interpret human behavior as a mere functional translation into action of neurobiological messages. Seen this way, needs are reduced to biology. Elsewhere, through the cultural innovations promoted by the feminist, environmentalist, and youth movements of the last twenty years, a definition of needs has emerged which treats them as the expression of a nature that resists or rebels against the social. The spontaneity of primary needs is put to stand in opposition to a society which obstructs or represses them with its apparatuses of control. The media, too, especially through advertising, have joined in ringing the appeal to natural needs by broadcasting the message of a good nature to which we should all return: the natural goodness embodied in the products that are advertised has only to be bought in order for one to achieve happiness, beauty, and well-being. Around this myth new markets have been developed and new styles of living and consumption created.

But the current notion of needs has also another and apparently contradictory side which assigns them to the relational systems of which we are part. The culture of the big organizations on the one hand, and the educational, psycho-social, and therapeutic services on the other, are increasingly pervaded by a hypersocialized image of needs as an expression of social and communicative processes. According to this perspective, we can work, be informed, educated, and treated only as part of a system of social relationships (families, friendships, associations, organizations). Family therapy, group work, team building and communicative training are rapidly transforming into new myths and becoming binding social rules which govern our life in all its dimensions: affection, work, religion, schooling, leisure. As individuals, in order to be able to recognize our needs, we should be reintegrated into the communicative networks within which those needs are formed. The group becomes the obligatory ground rule to which we must adhere if we are to know who we are. This emphasis on the social dimension of needs is also evident in the many forms of social participation and activism which seek to provide assistance to the socially deprived (the poor, the old, the handicapped, drug addicts, those who are sick). Here society is accused of neglecting the social nature of needs, and the agencies of social regulation are criticized for reducing needs to their purely individual dimension and not taking care of their social roots in inequality and marginalization.

The fact that needs are represented in such antithetical ways is nevertheless not a contradiction. Rather, it expresses a profound redefinition of our cultural field. The words with which we define our needs conceal a void, even as these definitions invade public and private discourse. Behind them lies a multiplicity of meanings which expresses the ambivalence of the nature and the sociability which constitute us. We are no longer able to identify our needs univocally. They are part of a symbolic field charged with tensions: an arena where the feelings of lack, absence, and weakness which continue to fuel our search for answers clashes with the power we have acquired over ourselves and over our environment. Fragile and creative, agonized by our wants and tempted by omnipotence, we live with our needs as a domain sometimes clear, sometimes confused, now safe, now fraught with danger.

Appeal to nature is the strategy with which we resist external pressure, the logic of efficiency and calculation, and the obligation to communicate at any cost. When we define our needs as natural, they have for us the opacity and consistency of something already given. We use naturalness of needs to counteract the pressures that seek to integrate us into social rhythms by coercion, and we believe we can use them to escape from the incessant communication that an information society requires of us. In a confused manner, the appeal to nature also expresses the idea of our natural existence as a field of action, as something that we can produce rather than something that is already given. We have begun to consider our bodies, our biological structure, and our sexuality as parts of ourselves – parts which can become domains of our personal freedom and intervention.

However, evoking the natural basis of our needs also feeds to the illusion that it is possible to withdraw from social relations. It induces us to reject – sometimes to a pathological extent – the constraints that we must respect as social actors. The first of these constraints is a consequence of the fact that the resources available to us are scarce and unequally distributed. Such inequality no longer concerns the material resources alone, for scarcity now increasingly involves other dimensions of experience as well: time, information, and affectivity. Furthermore, in order to act at all we still have to estimate the expediency of our actions, and in so doing we are compelled to respect, to some extent, the imperatives of efficiency and effectiveness. Finally, we live within power relations which remain impossible for us to ignore (although they can be modified) and which we must accept as a condition of our associative life.

A naturalistic conception of needs therefore tends to lure us into the false belief that these constraints can be evaded. It conjures up a transparent world where spontaneous needs can be satisfied, were it not for the repressive control of the society.

On the other hand, an appeal to the sociality of needs may become an instrument of social control as it easily lends itself to the purposes of forced integration of the individual into the group. However, it none the less expresses the profound need to communicate and to relate with others, a need so frequently denied us by the fragmented and atomized way of life of mass society. It declares, moreover, that our personal needs are also political: they are directed towards the *polis* and they must be recognized if we are to participate in civil life. Lastly, by proclaiming the social rootedness of our needs we seek to resist the process of individualistic reduction, the fragmentation, the bureaucratic-administrative specialization that those agencies which attend to our education, health, affective relations, and aging impose on them.

When we celebrate the assumed spontaneity of needs, or, alternatively, when we socialize them by force, we reduce them to just one of the two poles: we deny their inherent ambivalence as something stretched between nature and society. Whether within or without us, nature has ceased to be the realm of obscure forces: it now responds to our conscious action. But none the less it continues to set limits on such action and it is still the arena where we resist external pressures. In turn, our cultural elaboration of needs circumscribes nature with social rules and language, and confines it within the constraints of our relations. It thus enables us to transform energy into information and to acculturate the nature that constitutes us.

We can no longer conceive of our needs as compelling and instinctual urges, or as transparent manifestations of a benevolent nature that guides us. But nor can we continue to labour under the illusion that nature can be substituted by a society to which we assign the task of instructing us or which we accuse of repression. Needs are a signal of something that we lack, and it is up to us to recognize these needs and to give them cultural expression. Thereby we are, moreover, called to assume a responsibility which we cannot evade: we must become able to respond consciously to the perception of the lack that constitutes us. In other words, we must learn to decide who we are and want to be.

Identity?

The experience of something lacking thus compels us to ask who we are; and any attempt for an answer leads us to probe the question of our identity. Although in everyday language the term 'identity' accommodates a variety of meanings, it is most commonly used to refer to three phenomena: the permanence over time of a subject unaffected by environmental changes below a certain threshold level; the notion of unity, which establishes the limits of a subject and enables us to distinguish it from all others; and a relation between two elements which enables us to recognize them as identical.

We may talk of the identity of a person or of a group, but in both cases we make a reference to those three features – namely, continuity of the subject over and beyond variations in time and its adaptations to the environment; the delimitation of this subject with respect to others; and the ability to recognize and to be recognized.

It is difficult to talk of our identity without at the same time referring to its relational and social roots. This is a problem which has been central to the recent debates in the neurological and cognitive sciences examining what is innate to human behavior and what are its acquired elements. Extreme positions have been developed, but as a whole the prevailing trend seems to be to adopt the intermediate view that the relational and social aspects of identity are embedded within its biological constitution itself. As regards the brain, for instance, heredity would transmit a neuronal programme which governs the growth of an individual's nervous system. The programme creates conditions under which individual differentiation unfolds as a result of interaction with the environment. Selection mechanisms shape every development process, and the brain 'forms' itself (in the literal sense of the word) until it has acquired a stable capacity to respond and adapt to environmental stimuli. At the end of this maturation phase, the brain has learned to respond consistently to same kinds of stimuli. Simultaneously, it develops a plasticity to shape itself to new circumstances and to perform new functions.

Psychological and sociological research confirms that individual identity develops in a circular relationship with a system of constraints. Individuals are able to identify themselves when they have acquired the ability to distinguish between themselves and the environment. Studies in genetic psychology and symbolic interactionism which investigate the early structuring of identity have demonstrated the crucial role of primary interactions – the processes of recognizing and being recognized – in the most deep-seated formative experiences of the life of an infant. Moreover, one need not accept the entire edifice of Freudian metapsychology in order to acknowledge the decisive contribution of psychoanalysis in revealing the relational bases of identity. In addition, the advances in both clinical theory and modern theories of communication have shown that while relations structure identity, relational breakdowns destructure it. Thus, modern social sciences have forcefully advanced the idea that the individual and the system reciprocally constitute each other, and that a subject only becomes aware of itself as a subject through her/his active interchanges with an external environment and through the resources/constraints offered by it.

Identity thus defines our capacity to speak and to act autonomously – the differentiation of our selves from those of others while continuing to be the same person. However, self-identification must still gain intersubjective recognition if it is to provide the basis for identity. Our ability to distinguish ourselves from others must be acknowledged by those very same 'others'. Therefore our personal unity, which is produced and maintained by self-identification, rests on our membership in a group and on our ability to locate ourselves within a system of relations. No one can construct her/his identity independently of its recognition by others. Every individual must assume that her/his otherness and uniqueness is constantly acknowledged by everyone else and that this recognition is based on intersubjective reciprocity ('I am for You the You that You are for Me').

Hence it is impossible to draw a rigid distinction between the individual aspects of identity on the one hand, and its relational and social aspects on the other. In a person's life-history, identity is a learning process which is consummated in the emergence of the autonomous subject. As we pass through the various stages of our life, we develop a capacity to resolve the problems posed by the environment and become increasingly independent in constituting our relationships. The internalization of the cultural universe of our society together with our capacity to give a cultural interpretation of our needs substitutes our 'natural' dependence on the environment: first as an integration with this symbolic universe, then as a process of individuation whereby we acquire sufficient independence from the system so as to be able to produce autonomously what we formerly had to obtain from others. Adult identity can therefore be described as the ability to produce new identities by integrating the past and the choices available in the present into the unity and continuity of the individual life-history. Learning does not end with adolescence: as we pass through the various stages of life that follow it, we continue to question and reformulate our identities.

It is above all in situations of crisis that our identity and its weaknesses are revealed – as for instance when we are subjected to contradictory expectations, or when we lose our traditional bonds of belonging, when we join a new system of norms. These conflicts constitute a severe test for our identity, and they may also damage it. In such situations, we can respond by restructuring our action according to new orientations. Or, alternatively, we can compartmentalize our spheres of life so that we can still preserve a degree (sometimes only an appearance) of coherence – if only internally in the case of each of these separate spheres in isolation. The most serious crises may provoke a breakdown, a fragmentation of the self, or a breach of its confines. This triggers a pathology; that is, an incapacity to produce and maintain a definition of the self which could exhibit a certain stability; or, vice versa, a forced assumption of a rigid identity from which it is impossible to escape.

'Identity' is therefore above all the autonomous ability to produce and to recognize the self. Such a definition, however, is paradoxical, for it implies that we both perceive ourselves as similar to others (and are therefore able to recognize ourselves and be recognized at the same time) and also affirm our differences as individuals. The paradox of identity is that difference, in order to be affirmed and experienced as such, presupposes a degree of equality and reciprocity.

We can also talk of collective identity as the identity which ensures the continuity and permanence of the group or the society to which we belong.

Over time, identity establishes the limits of a group with respect to its natural and social environment. It determines the membership of the individuals, it defines the requirements for joining the group, and the criteria by which its members recognize themselves and are recognized. The content of this identity and its temporal duration vary according to the type of the group or the society concerned. We know today that in the transition from traditional to modern industrial society the site of the identification processes gradually shifted from outside of society to its interior, from gods and ancestors to actual social relationships. The foundations of identity in traditional societies were always metasocial; they lay in the mythical time of origin or coincided with the holy figure of the chief. The desacralization of the roots of identity has relocated the sources of identification processes inside the society itself, within the networks of associative human action. As identity has been progressively recognized as socially produced, so have also the conditions been created for the individuation of the processes of attribution and recognition. It is we as individuals who increasingly are offered the chance to acquire the autonomous capacity to define ourselves as individuals.

Notions like coherence, limit maintenance, recognition, and reciprocity describe identity in static terms; but in its dynamic connotation our identity is a process of individuation and increasing autonomy. Today, identity is the product of our conscious action and the outcome of self-reflection more than a set of given or inherited characteristics. It is we ourselves who construct our coherence and recognize ourselves within the limits set by the environment and social relations. Our identity tends to coincide with conscious processes of individuation; we experience it not so much as a situation as an action. The word 'identity' itself is inadequate to express this change; we should instead talk of *identization* to express the processual, self-reflexive, and constructed manner in which we define ourselves.

Continuing however to use the term in its customary sense, we may speak of identity as the ability to recognize as ours the effects of our actions, and therefore as the ability to attribute these effects to ourselves. Thus defined, identity presupposes, first, that we are able to reflect on ourselves. Our action is not simply a reaction to biological and environmental constraints; it produces symbolic orientations and meanings which we are able to recognize. Secondly, it entails that we have a notion of causality and belonging; that, in other words, we are able to attribute the effects of our actions to ourselves, establishing a link between the actor and her/his action. This recognition underpins our ability to appropriate the outcomes of our actions, to exchange them with others, and to decide how they should be allocated. It is therefore the foundation of our responsibility. Thirdly, identity entails an ability to perceive duration, an ability which enables us to establish a relationship between past and future and to connect action to its effects. Only if these conditions are met are we able to talk about ourselves as constituting a self that endures over time.

If it is true that our identity is formed only within a set of social relations, and if it is true that identity can develop only in interaction and through reciprocal recognition between us and others, then identity contains an unresolved and unresolvable tension between the definition we give of ourselves and the recognition accorded to us by others. Identity thus entails a gap between self-identification and identification by others.

When we find ourselves involved in an exchange, this discrepancy and the tension provoked by it are partly kept under control by a certain level of reciprocity of recognition. The exchange is based on the recognition in ourselves of that which we recognize in the (equal/different) other, and vice versa, at least within certain limits which never imply a total reciprocity and transparency. However, there are situations where this may become impossible: individual differences, diversity or inequality of social positions, the timing of giving and receiving in exchange relations, may increase the distance between us and others. Reciprocity proves impossible, competition for scarce resources begins, and a situation of conflict arises.

The tension between auto-identification and hetero-identification by the Other erupts into conflict when both of the subjects involved deny each other their identities. Each of them is part of the relationship but refuses to grant the other the recognition s/he demands. The conflict disrupts the reciprocity of the interaction; the opponents clash over something which is common to both of them but which each withholds from the other. Beyond the concrete or symbolic objects at stake in a conflict, what people struggle for is always the possibility to recognize themselves and be recognized as subjects of their own action. We enter a conflict to affirm the identity that our opponent has denied us, to reappropriate something which belongs to us because we are able to recognize it as our own.

When during a conflict we secure solidarity from others, when we feel ourselves part of a group, identity is reinforced and guaranteed. We feel a bond with others not chiefly because we share the same interests, but because we need this bond in order to make sense of what we are doing. The solidarity that ties us to others enables us to affirm ourselves as subjects of our action and to withstand the propensity for breakdown in social relations induced by conflict. Moreover, we learn how to gather and focus our resources in order to reappropriate that which we recognize as ours. Participation in forms of collective mobilization or in social movements, involvement in modes of cultural innovation, voluntary action inspired by altruism – all these are grounded in the need for securing our identity and facilitate its satisfaction.

Today's collective conflicts increasingly express a public concern for recognition, making manifest a group-based social struggle to secure recognition of identity at the societal level: they transfer into the public arena a definition of needs and identity which is originally built in every-day life experiences and networks. In so doing, they transform identity issues into visible political stakes and they bring into the field of decision-making and rights the tension mentioned above between auto-identifica-tion and hetero-identification (recognition). On the one hand, through their claims they disclose the new potential for autonomous identification that is made available at the societal level by highly differentiated and complex systems. In this respect, the collective conflicts in the contemporary society address the societal field as such and they name it openly also for the rest of the society. On the other hand, by the particularism of their auto-identification process they expose themselves to the constant risk of a seg-regated identity, unable to cope with the responsibility that recognition implies – namely, the fact that we need to be recognized by others in order to affirm ourselves.

Field and process

To sum up, we cannot treat our identity as a 'thing', as the monolithic unity of a subject; instead, it should be conceived as a system of relations and representations. We possess several different identities of varying degrees of complexity – personal, family, social, and so on – the difference being the particular system of relationships to which we refer: the system which conveys to us the recognition.

In every case identity is a relation which embraces both our ability to rec-ognize ourselves and the possibility of being recognized by others. This polarity between auto-recognition and hetero-recognition falls along the two dimensions which were previously indicated as constitutive of identity: unity and difference. On the one hand, we proclaim who we are; that is, we affirm 'I am X or Y'. By so doing, we declare the continuity and the perma-nence of our being, expecting it moreover to be recognized by others. This dimension we may call 'identification'. On the other hand, we distinguish ourselves from others and we seek recognition of such diversity. This we may call 'the affirmation of difference'.

Our identity therefore takes the form of a quadripolar field containing a system of vectors in tension. These vectors constantly seek to establish an equilibrium between the identification that we declare of ourselves and the identification that is accorded by others, or the difference we ourselves affirm and the difference that is recognized by others.

Our identity in its concrete everyday form depends on how successfully and consistently this set of relations is held together: how we recognize ourselves and affirm our diversity, how we internalize the recognition granted by others, and how they define our difference. This system is never a definitive datum; it is instead a laborious process where unity and equilibrium are reestablished in reaction to shifts and changes in the elements internal and external to the field. Our identity therefore takes its particular form according to the presence and relative strength of each of its constitutive dimensions. We may imagine it as a field which expands and contracts, with its borders changing in accordance with the varying intensity and direction of the forces that constitute it.

Some vectors may be weaker or stronger than others, and some of them may be entirely absent. For example, when we identify ourselves and affirm our difference without this being recognized by others, or when such recognition is only half-hearted, our identity is severed from the relation and becomes a *segregated* identity. In its normal form, this occurs in certain phases of adolescence when rebellion against the adult world aggravates the need for separate identification. Examples of a similar pattern at the collective level are to be found in the formative stage of movements, in marginal countercultures, and in sects. In individual pathology, the hypertrophic development of a narcissistic ego or exaggerated withdrawal into the self are further examples of such a pattern of behaviour.

In other cases, we are identified and recognized as different by others, but our own ability to recognize ourselves as such is weak. Here identity is *other-directed* and manifests itself in deferential conduct, crowd behaviour, and certain forms of gregarious tendencies, as well as in the exaggerated tendency to embrace the opinions and expectations of others. Other-direction in its normal form is characteristic of certain phases of child development, and is gradually left behind as the personality develops. In its pathological form, it degenerates into a morbid symbiosis or attachment which hinders the growth of an autonomous capacity for identification.

Yet another pattern is provided by the situation in which we are capable of identifying ourselves autonomously, while our diversity is fixed by others. This we could term *labelled* identity, with the processes of social labelling exemplifying the most evident ways in which it is produced. Our sexual, racial, and cultural differences and our physical or behavioural handicaps are stigmatized as non-social attributes. This stunts our autonomous capacity for identification as we internalize the label that has been socially imposed on us.

When we lack the capacity to create our own definition, we take on a *deviant* identity, and thus define ourselves solely in terms of our diversity. Here the norms and models of behaviour are lived as if they were entirely assigned to us by others. Our inability to adopt and internalize them owing to some failure of the socialization process, however, forces us to reject them by exaggerating our diversity. We are in reality what others tell us we are; indeed, the model they provide for us is our only identification but only one external, that we are unable to transform in autonomous personal values. Since it is impossible to realize this model positively, we do it by negation. Shoplifting is the reverse side of consumerism, just as self-destructive drug abuse or alcoholism shows the reverse side of the over-ambitious expectations we are unable to fulfil.

Conflicts always express the opposition between the two poles of auto-recognition and hetero-recognition, between the way we define ourselves and the way others define us. As I argued before, every conflict (even when a concrete object, like a material good is at stake) also involves a conflict of identity. The poles of identity disconnect; the equilibrium breaks down between the definition we give of ourselves and the definition attributed to us by others. Our opposition to, and clash with, the 'other' is an attempt to affirm the relation, a means to reestablish the nexus between the different poles of identity – a way to rebuild the conditions of exchange necessitating reciprocal recognition. In sum, it is then within and through conflict that we realize that our identity is relational and that the tensions between the self and the other cannot be overcome.

Living in a differentiated and rapidly changing society, we belong to numerous systems of relations and perpetually move among them in time and space during our life course. Establishing an equilibrium between the different vectors along which our identity is constructed becomes progressively more difficult, and there is an increased likelihood of 'identity crisis', as a result of the inability to maintain a coherent spatio-temporal pattern of the definition of our selves. As a consequence, conflicts – both interpersonal and those between groups (generations, genders, cultures) – also become more probable. To meet these challenges, identity tends to lose its stable contents and to transform itself into a purely symbolic capacity to recognize oneself.

The discontinuity and fragmentation of experience engendered by complexity dissolves the 'subject', understood as an essence with permanent characteristics. The phenomenon of the 'homeless mind', the rootlessness of personality which has been pointed to as typical of contemporary societies, not only signals a crisis but also signifies that identity is in the process of being redefined as a pure self-reflexive capacity or self-awareness. We can progressively fill with mutable contents the empty form that this capacity in effect is, and live our continuity in the present through the symbolic capacity to recognize ourselves as being the 'actors' and 'authors' of our action, in the original sense of these terms. Subject to the increasingly diversified flow of experience, we can preserve our 'substance' – the continuity between the past and the present and between the many social fields which constantly force us to define ourselves in different ways – only if we recognize in ourselves that formal and unique capacity for action which identifies us as distinct individuals in relation to other people. And this recognition can only emerge as a conscious experience of being present to ourselves and to the world: that presentness which makes us feel simultaneously unique and connected to the others and to the cosmos.

Identity breakdowns

If the delicate balance among the poles of identity is upset, if the process of continuous adjustment falters, we suffer anguish and the loss of self. In highly differentiated and mutable social systems, the self is exposed to a number of pressures; the reverse side of a broader potential for autonomy and freedom is the risk of identity breakdowns. We may not be able to meet the challenge of constructing an autonomous definition of ourselves or in trying to do so may be pushed to the border of what is considered to be socially acceptable behaviour. Never before has society been so concerned with defining normality and pathology. The issue features prominently in contemporary medicine, psychiatry and psychology, but it concerns a far broader area of social behaviour. At stake is essentially a question of deciding what makes individuals autonomous agents of their own action. Or, conversely, of what prevents them from recognizing themselves, and being recognized as subjects, and from acting autonomously. Madness represents a kind of reversed mirror of our relationship with identity.

More than ever before, madness interrogates our culture and the ways 'normality' is defined. The history of madness is a history of this interrogation, but today the answers we give for its disquieting presence are beginning to develop radically new connotations. When the content and confines of individual identity increasingly depend on our capacity to define them, rather than on external social rules, the borderline between what is 'normal' and what is 'pathological', instead of indexing a clinical/nosographic demarcation of naturally existing categories, becomes blurred and thus a subject matter of societal debates and confrontations.

In the eighteenth century, the introduction of the lunatic asylum flanking the prison system marked the birth of mental illness as a distinct condition monitored and treated by a team of specialists. The medical profession separated 'illness' from criminality, isolating it as a specific form of misbehaviour within the general category of poverty. Poverty was considered a culpable condition, a mark of those individuals who were unable to commit themselves to the 'industrious classes' and had consequently gravitated towards the 'dangerous classes'. Along with criminal behaviour, but set apart from it, mental illness became one of the visible signs of this corrupt condition, and it was relegated to the jurisdiction of a specialized sector of health care profession. Bourgeois sanity had to be safeguarded against the underclasses, whose handling called for various different measures: the prison and charity were now accompanied by the lunatic asylum that combined the features of both its predecessors. By establishing a norm which satisfied the criteria of the bourgeois rationality, early psychiatry constructed a scientific edifice which defined and classified mental illness, while segregating off the institutions where it was treated.

The history of psychiatry is of course not wholly coterminous with the rise of bourgeois mental hygiene and its accompanying notion of rationality, nor can it be simply identified with the emergence of the lunatic asylum as an institution. Psychoanalysis brought significant changes to psychiatric methods, and the insights of neurology clarified a number of organic aspects of mental illness. However, up until the 1940s the lunatic asylum was the central pillar of the social treatment of madness, as well as the principal tool of psychiatry as a 'scientific' discipline assigned for the task of treating the mentally ill.

After the Second World War, the spread of welfare models brought about a major change in the treatment of madness (as well as many other social problems, such as sickness, old age, criminality). The reorganization of health care provision dispensed with the institutions of total segregation, and now took upon itself to treat deviance by seeking to integrate the patient into the social fabric. Pathological behaviour was no longer seen as an individual problem, and treatment shifted its focus on to the network of social relations in which the fountainhead of the disorder could be diagnosed. Attention thus moved from intrapersonal factors to the social and relational causes of deviant behaviour.

Psychiatric treatment, or care in the broad sense, has subsequently expanded in scope and multiplied. It is now finely interwoven with the whole fabric of everyday public and private life. We have largely – even if not completely – left behind the violence of the institutions of segregation, but as clients of the service apparatus we have now become tightly integrated into a circuit of welfare dependence. The range of the administrative powers of the welfare services covers the entire span of our day-to-day existence. Deviance is treated through administrative channels, and social problems are reduced to a myriad of 'files' and 'cases' circulating through the network of the various specialists concerned.

Among the factors that contributed to these changes was also the critique of the psychiatric institution in modern psychiatry that sought to renew the very bases of psychiatric treatment by recasting the scientific and institutional definition of mental illness. During the 1960s and 1970s a part of institutional psychiatry fought against the violence of the asylum and tried to humanize the treatment of the patients, putting at the same time into question the scientific basis on which the old model was based. With regard to the closedness, rigidity, and archaic management patterns of the lunatic asylum, its critics denounced the inhumanity of the psychiatric institution and disclosed the connection between mental illness and social organization. The most advanced experiences for deinstitutionalization changed the criteria governing confinement and therapy in lunatic asylums: the inmates had their civil rights partly restored and were gradually returned to a form of civil life. The redefinition of mental health care enlarged not only the autonomy of its recipients but also lent a new professional identity to its practitioners. The treatment of suffering therefore became identical and contemporaneous with the restitution to the individual of her/his social autonomy. With the removal of the codified definition of illness imposed by traditional psychiatric theory, it became possible to consider the 'sick person' as a full person instead of just a 'case' (it is worth noting that the same word indicates both a medical case and a box to be filled for the classification according to nosographic categories).

These changes that were brought about by innovative psychiatric techniques and accompanied by debate and large-scale mobilization, made possible the reform of the lunatic asylum in many countries. However, the abandonment (or humanization) of the lunatic asylum – although a major step forward in the civil rights situation – did not eliminate the contradictions in the relationship between society and madness. In complex societies, also as a consequence of the reforms promoted by critical psychiatry, confinement to asylums is substituted by a widespread tendency to absorb an individual's adaptation problems into a network of social and medical services, and to assign treatment to a highly differentiated range of agencies which split pathology up along a variety of specializations. This in turn sets in motion an ambivalent process which may increasingly medicalize and fragment mental illness, and which could terminate in a disregard for the relational and social dimension of mental disorder and the actual suffering of the individual.

A widespread network of specialized services may provide a more effective and focused care, but it might adversely affect a ready labelling of any behaviour which does not conform to the dominant social rules. It may substitute the sick person's real social bonds as a member of the community with medical and professionalized relations internal to the system of welfare services: it may transfer psychological malaise and emotional trouble away from the realm of ordinary human experience to the domain of medical care. All the problems that the relationship between normality and pathology raises remain thus unsolved.

In light of this ambivalent development of mental health policies, what can madness tell us about our identity? How can we safeguard our right to look after ourselves against a medical practice which treats us as sheer objects? What is the place of therapy in a society which shows a tendency to 'cure' everything that it sees as different? Today, it is generally recognized that the social conditions of pathology and the individual difficulties connected with developing and maintaining an autonomous identity stand in a circular relationship. The conscious construction of identity (auto-identification) is recognized as necessary for an individual to be able to establish a social bond and to take up a position as one of the poles of interaction in such a relation. However, deep personal obstacles to auto-identification persist (genetic and related to primary affective experiences) which may cause the individual to be cut off from any relationship with reality. The social causes of psychiatric illness (marginalization, inadequate socialization, stigmatization or labelling) also raise obstacles for auto-identification. The breakdown of exchange relations that they precipitate isolates the individual in a phantasm world to the extent that s/he is withheld recognition by others. The lack of reciprocity in identification (I recognize myself and am recognized/I recognize myself and recognize the other) is therefore an outcome which always depends on the meeting of both of the twin poles of the self-other relation.

Madness is thus a multiple phenomenon, and it always stands at the intersection of the two vectors on the individual/society axis. We know nowadays a great deal more about the personal obstacles to the assumption and maintenance of identity. Research in biology, clinical psychology, and the neurosciences has shed light on the processes governing breakdown in the deep structure of the personality. We have also acquired new knowledge on the pathology induced by disturbances in family relations, by exclusion processes, and by the social labelling of those who are different. The two extreme cases represented by this axis are manifested as a pure individual

inability to construct an identity on the one hand, and pure social stigmatization of socially unacceptable behaviour on the other. Actual cases of
mental disorder always lie somewhere in between.

Every form of therapy therefore proceeds as an irreducible dialectic
between emancipation and control. Therapy responds to individual needs
on a mandate given to it by society. In setting out to relieve an individual's
suffering, therapy invariably applies, to a greater or lesser extent, the code
of normality which predominates in the particular culture. The ambivalence of its status is irremediable. Opting for the emancipation of the
patient (user/sick person/deviant) does not in fact free therapy from the
logic of control.

Whether or not contact can be maintained between the poles of the
ambivalence without their becoming neutralized in the process depends on
the theory and practice of therapy. The more violent and heteronomous the
therapy, the greater the exercise of control and repression, and the more
evident the normalization of the subject back to a social code (regardless
of whether or not the therapy is ideologically described as 'liberation').
Therapeutic treatment which is not governed by respect for the patient and
her/his own responsibility for a better-being becomes an orthopaedic
operation on social relations – the bending of the individual to the social
norm. Conversely, respect for the patient's individuality, for her/his
responsibility in following one's own path, may help to promote individual
autonomy.

Modern psychiatry has to make practical decisions in a very close relation to these issues. It must choose between, on the one hand, the increasing use of psychotropic medication, the direct or indirect manipulation of
the cerebral nerve centres, as the more or less explicit conditioning of
behaviour; and, on the other hand, the search for new therapeutic instruments which make patients responsible for healing themselves and constructing an autonomous identity. The issues raised by madness thus cast
revealing light on those numerous sectors of social life, medical and otherwise, where our needs are addressed and instruments of normalization
applied.

The ambivalence of therapy derives from the way that our culture defines
normality and pathology. Emancipation and control, sanity and madness,
are in reality contrasting definitions of the same phenomenon; they are the
cultural codes which our language uses to speak of the capacity to make
sense of action. The categories 'sanity' and 'normality' indicate that there
exists a social order which imposes its rules, but also the fact that we have
an autonomous ability to give meaning to what we do. 'Madness' and
'pathology' express the loss of such meaning, but at the same time they also

serve as witness to the fact that there is an alternative to the dominant form of sanity, a difference which cannot be reduced to the rules of social conformity.

Normality is therefore the responsible exercise of our capacity for action and the conscious construction of our identity. Yet, it is also dependence on the rules that govern society. Madness reminds us that the meaning of the possible is never completely encapsulated by the social order. Hence, to speak of madness is always to speak of ourselves and of our ambivalence.

3

Metamorphosis of the
multiple self

Nomads of the present

Ever since its advent, the modern world has offered individual action an open field of possibility. The myths of progress and liberty have fed the Promethean dream of freeing mankind from natural constraints, by submitting nature to the dominion of technological power. Moreover, the promise of freedom has been extended to regard also the life of the individual, for whom it envisages an irresistible progress towards autonomy and full realization of the personal potential.

These ideas have constituted the historical framework of modernity in all its variants, whether rationalist or utopian, and, in spite of the vicissitudes of its career, this inheritance still encompasses the entire gamut of our hopes and our fears.

The scenario of complexity, of a system which by now irreversibly incorporates the whole planet and, to an equal measure, faces a future jeopardized by prospects of catastrophe, has deeply eroded the optimism of the myths of salvation. None the less, we still hold on to the most exalting and dramatic legacy of modernity: our need and duty to *exist as individuals*. We, namely, can think of ourselves as subjects of action capable of purposive and meaningful behavior, but at the same time we also function as the coordinates in a network of communality and communication.

Yet new dilemmas have arrived to beset the everyday lives of the children of disenchantment. In information societies our consciousness attains new levels of reflexivity. What matters today is no longer mere learning, but rather learning *how* to learn – how to control our cognitive and motivational processes and to adapt them to new problems. Technological power has been accompanied by an exponential growth of symbolic possibilities, by an increase in self-reflective activity: by the heightened capacity to reflect and represent reality through a multitude of languages. This capacity seems to be gradually replacing reality itself, so that we are in the process of coming to inhabit a world constructed out of the images that we ourselves have created, a world where we no longer can distinguish reality from the reality of the image.

We find ourselves enmeshed in multiple bonds of belonging created by the proliferation of social positions, associative networks, and reference groups. In simply conducting our lives, we enter and leave such systems far more frequently and in a far more rapid sequence than we did in the past. We have become migrant animals in the labyrinths of the metropolis, travellers of the planet, nomads of the present. In reality or in the imagination, we participate in an infinity of worlds. Each of these worlds, moreover, has a culture, a language, and a set of roles and rules to which we must adapt whenever we migrate from one of them to another. Thus we are subjected to mounting pressures to change, to transfer, to translate what we were just a moment ago into new codes and new forms of relation.

We transform ourselves into sensitive terminals, transmitting and receiving a quantity of information which far exceeds that seen in any previous culture. Our means of communication, our work environment, our interpersonal relationships, and even our leisure generate information addressed to individuals who must receive, analyze, and store that information in memory and almost always respond to it by producing further information.

The rhythm of change accelerates at an immense pace. The multiplication of our social memberships and the incessant surge of possibilities and messages flood the field of our experience. The traditional coordinates of personal identity (family, church, party, race, class) weaken. It becomes difficult to state with certainty that 'I am X or Y': the question 'Who am I?' presses with constant urgency for an answer. We are plagued by the fragility of a presentness which calls for a firm foundation where none exists; we search for permanent anchors, and we question our own life histories. Are we still who we were in the past? Can we still stay the same when we respond to what will be asked of us even tomorrow? We scan our pasts and our futures through different lenses as we move from one region of experience to another. In the age of speed, we no longer possess a home; we are repeatedly called upon to build and then rebuild one, like the three little pigs of the fairy tale, or we have to carry it along with us on our backs like snails.

Everyday time is multiple and discontinuous, for it entails the never-ending wandering from one universe of experience to another: from one membership network to another, from the language and codes of one social sphere to those of another, semantically and affectively very different from it. Time loses its formerly characteristic uniformity and begins to follow a variable rhythm imposed by the amount and the quality of the information we receive and transmit. Our perception alternatingly shrinks and expands, relaxes and intensifies, as we set off on our erratic migrations or are dragged along in them. We can no longer rely on the certainty of the end-directedness of time – the notion that modernity fed with its myths of progress and revolution. We, the bewildered witnesses of the demise of the great stories of salvation, are haunted by our new destiny of *choice*. To cope with the possible both seductive and threatening to us, we are compelled to assume all the risks that go with decision-making (of which catastrophe, nuclear or environmental, is the extreme image and metaphor).

The paradox of choice

Choosing is the inescapable fate of our time. Wherever it is we may physically reside, we are always and at the same time inhabitants of New York or Paris, London, San Francisco or Tokyo, of those real or imagined metropolises which constitute the terminals of an interdependent and highly complex planetary system. We cannot escape our symbolic inclusion in a cosmopolitan culture which expands and multiplies the possible worlds of our experience, while at the same time confronting us with their complexity and the necessity to make choices. Complexity signifies differentiation, high speed and frequency of change, and broadening of opportunities for action.

If the various fields of our experience become progressively differentiated and specialized, we shall not be able to transfer the patterns of action developed for one of them over to another. Whenever we move from one setting or system of relations to another, we know that experience gained elsewhere cannot be transposed as such to the new context, and that we must learn from the beginning again to cope with the new system's particular languages and rules. Variability, as another feature of complex systems, implies a frequency and an intensity of change unparalleled in any other society of the past. The difficulty of transferring the same pattern of action from one time to another is thus all the more pronounced, and we find ourselves unable to rely on our previously acquired abilities of problem-solving. Lastly, complexity provides opportunities that in their scope far exceed the effective capacity for action of individuals or groups. We are constantly reminded that the field of action laid out before us remains far wider than what can be conquered of it through the opportunities that we are actually able to seize.

In terms of everyday experience, the outcome of these processes is that *uncertainty* has become a stable component of our behaviour. We cannot move from one context to another and draw on what we have already acquired elsewhere; we cannot pass from one time to another and carry over for implementation what we already are or know from the past; we cannot act without choosing from the vast array of possible options without thereby letting some of them fall by the roadside and electing instead others for realization. We live with an increasingly large quota of uncertainty and we are often overwhelmed. What are we to do in a *different* context? How can we tackle a *new* problem? Or, more simply and generally, *what* are we to do, which choice should we make? Many of our routine tasks become exercises in problem-solving, compelling us to acquire information, study the instructions, and, in the end, make a choice.

The imperative that immediately arises from uncertainty is therefore the necessity to choose. We thus find ourselves caught up in the paradox in which choice becomes destiny: it is impossible not to choose among the options available in any situation. In order to act in the first place, we are forced to make choices – whenever we move from one system to another, whenever we pass from one time to another, whenever we simply act at all. The paradox lies in the fact that the extension of our actual life-chances – that is, of the range of individual autonomy expressed in the act of choosing associated with the idea of will and freedom – also entails the unavoidable *obligation* to choose. Even non-choice constitutes a choice, for it signifies rejecting an opportunity, which no less is one choice among the many.

This situation heightens the ambivalence intrinsic to every experience of change. Whenever we consider whether or not to introduce change, there is something in the present that we deem inadequate, something that does not satisfy us or that restricts us. Change, in other words, is a goal we find desirable and towards which our search for the new and the different is directed. But at the same time, change poses a threat to our security and to our established and habitual rules. Thus, when contemplating change, we are always torn between desire and fear, between anticipation and uncertainty. This highly risky and unpredictable game has no guaranteed success as its outcome; we may succeed, we may fail, but we are always exposed to the danger of losing ourselves in the process.

Consequently, the paradox of choice creates a new kind of psychological pressure, confronting us with new problems. Choosing among the multitude of possibilities is a difficult undertaking, and what we discard is always more than what we eventually choose. It is always accompanied by an inevitable sense of loss which itself stands in the background of numerous forms of depressive pathology. The endogenous depression of the psychiatry manuals is really the pure experience of loss without a distinct object.

A different but complementary reaction to the pressure of choice can be observed in the attempt to secure all the options simultaneously. On one hand, the self may split as it seeks to deny the partial nature of every choice; disconnecting the fragments and recreating each of them in a separate totality allows the illusion of not having to choose – and lose – at all. One can pass from one fragment to another, denying the mutual exclusiveness of the alternatives present at any moment, all of them by definition partial.

Or, on the other hand, we may come to know the manic syndrome manifested in the multiplication of our efforts to answer every call, forming into an endless spiral which eventually exhausts us.

The multiple self and responsibility

Even when our anxiety falls short of the extreme stage of psychic malaise, our self undergoes a profound process of transformation which multiplies its faces. Descriptions of the multiplicity of the self usually stress the variations of the self over time and the discontinuities among the identifications forced upon us by rapid change. Equally important, at least, is the multiplicity that derives from uncertainty and the paradox of choice. Our self simultaneously comprises a number of components, and the innermost aspect of uncertainty is structured precisely by the difficulty we experience in identifying with just one of them, and by the requirement that we must nevertheless do so in order to be able to act. Hence, not only it is difficult to maintain our identity over time and to state that we still are what and who we used to be; it is also, and possibly even more so, hard to decide at any particular moment which self among the many possible is the one that is ours.

It becomes thus understandable that identity should coalesce into a central problem of contemporary social life, and that the general processes I have noted also have repercussions on organized social practices and even on legal systems, the final level at which social change crystallizes into norms and institutions. For example, notions such as responsibility and punishability, which necessarily depend on the establishment or non-existence of identity, are today at the centre of intense socio-political debate, raising enormous issues for jurisprudence. This issue also opens up a whole new field for the definition of rights.

The multiple nature of the self forces us to abandon any static view of the idea of identity and examine instead the dynamic processes of identification. The concept of identity is a substantialist notion which refers to a permanent essence as the foundation of identification. Rather than conceiving a subject that is endowed with an essential nucleus defined quasi-metaphysically, we must direct our attention to the processes by which individuals construct their identities. Identity as a multiple self then becomes *identization*.

Secondly, the multiplication of the self calls for a recognition of the place of individual action in social life. In contemporary systems, the site where the meaning of action is constructed shifts to the individual, who thus becomes a social actor in the true sense of the word. In the societies of the past, the meaning of individual behaviour was always sought on some plane or other of reality lying above or below the individual – gods, nature, the kinship system, the state, class, or Society itself as a metaphysical entity. Today, individuals are endowed with greater resources with which to construct their own individuality, and social action involves us precisely as individuals because we have become capable of producing autonomously and recognizing the meaning of what we are doing. From the metaphysical notion of the individual subject, we then shift our attention to the processes that make individuals individuals, to the processes which enable each one of us to become an autonomous subject of action. The individuality of a multiple self thus becomes *individuation*.

Thus characterized, the identity of a self emerges more as a field than as an essence: no longer a metaphysical reality but a dynamic system defined by recognizable opportunities and constraints. Identity is both a system and a process, because the field is defined by a set of relations and is simultaneously able to intervene on itself and to restructure itself. Subsequently, two crucial and perplexing problems arise here: the continuity of the self, and the boundaries of the self. Synchronically, the problem is one of deciding where the subject of action begins and where it ends; diachronically, we must establish how this subject persists through time. If we continue to think in terms of states and essences, the continuing advance of differentiation processes, the frequency and intensity of change, and the excess of opportunities that characterize a global society render it impossible to pose these two key problems in a manner that permits their solution.

Within the framework of the traditional categories, the only way out of such an impasse is to dissolve the self and to eliminate the social actor. This way, identity acquires the character of the mere presentation of the self, of a masquerade, in effect a play acted out on the public stage which disguises a void behind the guise of each participant. Alternatively, we must once again attach ourselves to any guarantor of a stable nucleus at hand in the desperate attempt to reconstitute the lost essence – for example, by reviving primary bonds of belonging like kinship or local and geographical affinities. Such a reawakening of primary identities, the need to anchor oneself to something essential which shows permanency and has tangible referents, lies at the basis of many contemporary collective phenomena. Ethnic or geographical identification, the attachment to traditional culture, express the attempt to resist the dissolution of identity conceived as an essence.

These reactions, nevertheless, cannot counter the decline of an essentialist idea of identity, even if they apparently reawaken the strength of primary bonds. In fact, the cultural, territorial or ethnic legacy is symbolically reinterpreted and the search for a 'traditional' identity relies upon the resources of an information society. The very emergence of these collective phenomena confirms the dissolution of identity as an essence and calls for a new analytical frame: we should begin to conceive identity as a relational field comprising both freedoms and constraints. Only then can the problem of its boundaries and its permanence be recast. The boundaries of identity can be conceived of as the recognition of constraints and the interplay between their opening and closing. The problem of the continuity of identity can be recast as that of the continuity of forms; continuity or discontinuity is not detected in the comparison of contents, as if they were 'ontological states', but in the process-bound organization of various systems of relations.

This perspective leads us directly to the topic of responsibility. If identity is a process of identization, and if the individual coincides with her/his action of self-identification, the problem becomes that of defining who chooses how the field is to be organized, synchronically (who am I at this moment?) and diachronically (who am I compared with yesterday or tomorrow, compared with memory or my project?). The topic of responsibility becomes a crucial issue, and the term 'responsibility' itself should be taken in its most literal and profound sense as the *capacity to respond*.

If identity is no longer an essential nucleus or a metaphysical continuity, definition of its borders and maintenance of its continuity are entrusted to our capacity to respond – that is, to our ability to recognize and choose among the possibilities and constraints present in the field of relations that constitute us at any given moment. The very definition of the capacity to respond has a dual meaning: it comprehends *responding for* (answering for) and *responding to* (recognizing what we are and locating ourselves in our relations).

My responsibility towards that field of opportunities and constraints which constitutes 'I myself' is, on the one hand, a capacity to respond *for*, by assuming limitation, memory, biological structure, and personal history; on the other, it is the capacity to respond *to*, by choosing among opportunities and grasping them, by positioning myself in my relations with others and by taking my place in the world.

Metamorphosis and individuation

Identity, then, is a process involving constant negotiation among different parts of the self, among different times of the self, and among the different settings or systems to which each of us belongs. In its various components, identity considered as negotiation involves the capacity to respond to the multiplicity and contradictoriness of the elements of which we are composed at any given moment. As I act, my being never completely coincides with what I am doing. I choose and discard, I assign priority to some parts of myself over others, I remain partly unaware. My identity is the ability to bind all of this together, and my identity will be more conscious of itself the better it is able to negotiate among these various components and to bring them into existence in togetherness.

Negotiating among the various times of the self is assuredly a complicated project: here, too, different components of the whole must be held together. In this case, negotiation involves the constant adjustment of the temporal perspective and the ability to weave together memory and the project in the now-time. Lastly, our identity also comprises negotiation among different relational systems, or different levels of the self. What it is that we are depends not only on our intentions, but also on the social relations within which these intentions are set. Responsibility does not only concern the intentionality of the subject, but involves also the effects of our actions on the relational systems of which we are part, along with the restrictions that these place upon us. We are, therefore, also our relations, those which we accept and those which we reject, those that restrict us and those that enrich us.

Granting the emphasis on the aspect of negotiation, our identity appears to us as a process in which nothing is ever definitively lost and nothing ever definitively gained. It emerges as an experience of the self where the provisional and the reversible become constitutive of experience – not, however, in a sense that identity would be left precarious and fleeting as an achievement, but in the sense that it remains dependent on our choices. As social processes in today's society have increasingly shifted their centre towards the individual, a kind of subjectivization and interiorization of identity have taken place as a result. Yet this does not transform identity into a psychological construct, at least not in the reductive sense with which the term is often used. The construction of identity today involves our inner being for reasons that are profoundly social. Identity can be negotiated because there exist subjects of action who are no longer externally or objectively defined, but who themselves possess the capacity to produce and define the meaning of what they do.

There exists also a striking unequal distribution among parts of the world, its different groups and individuals, of the chances to construct an autonomous subject of action: these are the new 'structural' inequalities, the new 'class' imbalances of our time. This is the point where the deep 'individual' and 'subjective' dimension of identity reveals its 'social' and 'collective' nature.

It is the paradox of possibility as both limitless and ineluctable (we are unable not to choose) that has now for the first time clearly revealed the uniqueness of individual experience, the irresistible summoning of individuation. If time is no longer end-directed, it by definition becomes an unrepeatable construct, with every moment of it expanding to infinity. In itself, time carries no other meaning than the one that each of us is able to produce for him/herself, a meaning, however, which can provide a context for action only if it is shared with others.

Yet this situation does not relax the requirement of unity; it does not absolve us from the necessity to seek permanence in change. However, the continuity of individual experience can no longer be entrusted to any stable identification with a model, a group, a culture, or, perhaps, with a life history. It may appear, therefore, that the only quality minimally required of the inhabitants of the disenchanted world is the aridity of cynicism and detachment.

But in fact, no one is more caught in immobility than the cynic, and there is no greater rigidity than that of the detachment deployed to defend our undeclared fragility. The inhabitants of complexity have no need for this kind of cold-bloodedness; what we need is a passionate capacity *to change form*, to redefine ourselves in the present, to render choices and decisions reversible.

Metamorphosis is a response to a world which compels us to multiply our faces, languages, and relations. It is fundamentally a warm response, one not lacking in fear and anxiety, but likewise never lacking in love. Without compassion for oneself and for others, without hope or humility, the possibility to change form remains unattainable. What is otherwise left to be changed is but masks, the reliance (but for how long?) on the vacuous game of self-representation.

Standing at the point where numerous circuits of information intersect, at the junction of complex relational networks, the individual is in danger of being overwhelmed by noise, of being lacerated by the pressure of too many exchanges and too many desires. The threatened unity of the person can only be preserved by learning to *open up* and to *close down*, to move into and withdraw from the flow of messages, to resist the lure of the possible, to withstand the unhindered demands of the affections.

It subsequently becomes vital for each of us to find a rhythm to govern our entry to, and exit from, the relations that enable us to send and receive information, a rhythm with which we can resist losing the sense attached to the communication or the neutralization of its content.

Permanence and change

The very notion of identity reveals the weakness of our language when we deal with the critical changes of our time. Identity belongs to a constellation of concepts which are deeply embedded in the modern definition of the 'subject'. It is difficult to separate it from the idea of a substance or an essence of the self. Therefore this notion should be used very cautiously. While I do not find another, better term with which to substitute it, I am fully aware of the contradiction between the language I am using and what it is meant to address. Identity refers to continuity over time, to being equal to one's self and having definite boundaries, and it hardly applies to the processual dimension that an accelerated pace of change brings to the fore. In any case, the use of this concept helps to make clear that even in the conditions of an incessantly redefined process there is still the necessity of setting limits at any given time, a necessity felt by the individual and imposed or requested by the system.

There is therefore a permanent tension between the process of the continuous redefinition of oneself and the need to stabilize one's boundaries. Conceptually, it is important to shift from a consideration of identity in terms of either/or to a nonlinear perspective which includes the possibility of and/and. The back-and-forth between these perspectives depends on who asks the question of identity and from which point of view. The question can be asked by the individual, responding to the necessity of his/her internal unity; it can be raised by an external observer; it can convey the expectations of a system of relations to which the individual belongs and to which s/he has to respond. In all these cases the back-and-forth can take place, but with different stress on one side or another. For instance, when a system of relations is concerned (a family, a group, an organization) roles and reciprocal expectations delimit the possible definitions of one's identity, and the space available for negotiation and for change is limited by systemic boundaries. The more the system is structured and crystallized, the more individuals are defined by what the others expect from them. A model in terms of either/or could not account for these differences, and what we define as identity depends on the perspective we adopt and the capacity to shift our point of view.

The main implication of a nonsubstantialist idea of identity is that there must be someone who asks the question. Without this question being asked there is no problem of identity. Precisely who asks the question, matters for the answer which will be different in many ways according to whom it is directed. To respond to or to respond for, are dimensions of identity whose importance can vary depending on where the question originates.

Another important implication of a nonsubstantialist idea of identity is that the more we shift towards a processual definition, the more we will face the problem of how the very capacity of defining one's identity can be maintained. When identity is not perceived as a substantial essence any more, how can we assume the permanence of a subject of action who is able to define and recognize her/himself? In order to be able to cope with the transformations of identity, individuals need a formal capacity which is increasingly self-reflective and self-feeding over time. But the outcome of the process is not guaranteed any more; individuals are no longer ensured that they will be able to fulfil the task of setting boundaries and they do not know whether their definition will still be socially acceptable.

The continuity of identity should therefore increasingly rely not on specific contents but on what I would call personal capacity: a formal and processual capacity which enables the individual to assume a situational identity without a loss of a deeper sense of continuity of her/his personal existence. Personal capacity becomes very important but does not imply a separation of the individual dimension from social bonds. We do not always choose our ties, we are already part of systems of relations in which resources and constraints are given for individual existence. Even if much stress must be placed on the aspect of choice, I am fully aware of the fact that the fields to which we belong are already structured. There are recognition circles, structured systems in which certain values are recognized or certain resources can be spent. The same resources or values cannot be spent in other fields. But these fields can be interpreted by the actors with an increasing degree of autonomy, for individuals are provided with capacities to make sense of the social structures to which they belong.

Individuals contribute to the activation of their recognition circles, so that new exchanges, relations, and rituals are created within them. Recognition does not work automatically and is increasingly interactive. Without a certain individual capacity for negotiation, and without the establishment of certain procedures and rituals, the circle of recognition will not work by itself.

This opens a new field for identity entrepreneurs, social actors creating and selling the capacity for manoeuvring with identities; producing new opportunities for recognition, importing languages and codes from one field to another. This also explains why the definition of normality becomes a very critical matter for our society: who decides whether an identity is normal or pathological, and under which conditions? The issue is so critical because neither the individual alone, nor the society without individual participation and consent, can set the borders between normality and pathology. The sources of identity are increasingly individual, but for this very reason the social dimension of individual experience comes to the fore.

The boundaries of the present

Opening and closing become necessary capabilities if we are to preserve our unity in the flux of messages and in the interminable sequence of changes. In the alternation between noise and silence, we can create an inner space which persists even if languages and interlocutors change, and even when communication itself breaks down.

In order to be able to live with the discontinuity and heterogeneity of times and spaces, we are called to develop a capacity to unify experience other than that provided by instrumental reason. The passage from one time to another, fragmentation, and unpredictability cannot be captured by causal reasoning, by criteria based on efficiency, by the logic of rational calculation. What is required before all is the instant perception, the intuitive awareness, and the imagination, qualities to which traditional cultures always paid respect. Contemporary interest in the wisdom of these cultures is, beyond any fad or fashion, a significant sign of the need to unify experience according to a pattern that radically differs from the one conforming to instrumental rationality.

In order to endure change and to pass through the metamorphoses that characterize the modern life-course, our identity must be rooted in the present. We must be able to open and close our channels of external communication to keep our relations alive, yet without becoming submerged by the flood of messages in the process. We need new capacities for immediate and intuitive contact with reality, capacities that can assimilate an ever-expanding field of experience which resists confinement within the narrow limits of rational knowledge. We must therefore redraw the boundaries between inner and outer reality, and we must pay closer attention to our own selves, building the awareness that we exist as individual psycho-physical entities in relation with others and that we remain responsible for our choices. This self-reflective orientation would direct our personal quest towards a closer contact with inner experience.

We need multiple points of view to deal with the uncertainties of self-change, for without a capacity for perception and representation, without emotions, no new form of ourselves is possible. The rites of passage of traditional cultures ensured this change in the view of the self. But we can no longer rely on ritual protection as we confront the tests set for us by opportunity and constraint. The stages of the life-course, the great cadences of our biological and social cycles, are still there to remind us of the fact that regardless of how rich our possibilities may be, birth, growth, aging, and death are our inevitable destiny. It is our task, therefore, to find a form in which to pass through them.

The experience of transition, in the many passages of our daily lives or in the great passages of life, requires us to adopt a way of looking at ourselves which is not solely that established by Occidental reason. Art – which has always explored the avenues of change – can teach another way of looking at the self; it is not by chance that today creative activity is becoming for many a rewarding arena of personal inquiry. Also psychotherapy and other self-reflective and bodily practices related to the pursuit of a better-being represent today not just an answer to personal suffering: they often channel the need for a different rationality and represent a process through which to cope with the difficulties of transforming the self – another means by which form can be changed. What is common to these and other practices is the attempt to establish contact with an inner world detached from the fluctuating contents of experience.

The inner world of sensations, perceptions, and representations persists even though the sense impressions impinging upon it from the environment, along with the proprioceptive stimuli themselves, may change. This 'container' of personal experience, constituted by the pure awareness of our inner world and by our perceptual capacity, can assume different forms over time, but it is always perceivable in the here and now and can lend unity to different and contradictory elements of experience. The capacity of being present to oneself as a body, mind, and soul is the thread that stitches together the fragments of the individual life.

The body is the prime vehicle of presentness and of every communication. Opening and closing come about as the activation and disactivation of the senses in their contact with the outside. The body transmits and receives the basic messages (visual, auditory, kinesthetic) that give sense to communication. Closure, withdrawal from the world, or the cessation of communication, does not annul our presence to ourselves. The interior continues to be perceived, and this ensures our continuity and the possibility of further opening. Contact with the interior also leads to direct and intuitive perception, as the 'other' knowledge which integrates the disparate fragments of experience, the different times and the discontinuities between them. An awareness that also comprises information from the body, and which is as able to synchronize itself to the register of 'feeling' as it is to that of 'thinking', expands the field of consciousness. There are faculties and resources which operate naturally within the body as regulators of important biological functions. Their conscious activation shifts our entire perceptive experience into the field of consciousness and extends the range of possibilities available to us in our relationships with ourselves and the world.

An awareness which succeeds in incorporating in the now-time the broadest possible range of information without allowing itself to be submerged by it, an awareness that is able to 'see' without being dazzled, eases the passage from the outside to the inside, from the social time to the inner time, and vice versa. Fluency of the communication between these two dimensions of experience is certainly one condition for personal wholeness, whereas obstructions in the passage between them are commonly associated with a form of disorder or pathology. When our access to inner reality is impeded, we become trapped in the vacuous and repetitive game of social masks. On the other hand, the overtaxing labour of breaking out of the incommunicable circle of inner experiences may confine us into a prison of silence.

The definition and the perception of boundaries opens up two paths for us: one leading to communication with the outside (where the rules of social time must be respected); the other leading to our inner life that speaks our own secret language. In this coming and going, there is nothing of the necessary causal relation between the deep-lying level and the outer surface (or vice versa) which the determinism of nineteenth-century thought has rehearsed us to tacitly assume: determinism of the hidden world of instincts, or the determinism of the social order in its conditioning effect on individual consciousness. There is, instead, a circular pattern of relationships driving a dynamic process. Inner experience and social experience influence each other reciprocally. Human action does not come about as a consequence of the uncontrollable impact of internal forces (instincts, urges) on the normality of everyday time (as Freud would have put it). Rather, it is the result of the ongoing process of redefinition of innerness: the elements accumulated through social experience and the cultural data modify our perception and awareness of inner reality. Thus a cyclical pattern of opening and closure – the recurrent shuttling between the two planes of experience and among the various times of which they are composed – forms in our personal level of experience. Each of us becomes increasingly an arbiter and a regulator of the rhythm of these passages; only we are able to establish the tempo of the switches which mark the dynamic evolution, the metamorphosis of personal life.

The delicate interface between inner and outer reality is the point of contact where internal and external signals meet. Each one of us must decode these signals to be able to position ourselves with respect to the change of self and its impact on the world. When the field of possibilities expands beyond a certain scope, the problem of boundaries becomes the crux of individual and collective life: it covers under its aspects the problem of choice, uncertainty, and risk which renews in the hypertechnological scenario of the complexity the human experience of limitation – and of freedom. Where to put our boundaries is still the challenge that human life has to meet, when social power reaches the capacity for self-destruction and individual life relies on choices without guarantees. Setting our boundaries becomes today a matter of conscious and free acceptance of our limits.

Changing form requires fluidity of transition, an ability to retain and to let go accepting the loss, the generosity of risk and the prudence of limitation. The cold calculating rationality that has conditioned the modern experience of the West is ill-suited to this requirement. New qualities are required which we are just beginning to learn. Passing from one form to another without bursting apart, binding together the fragments of the unpredictable, entails a capacity for intuition and imagination which has always been banished to segregated enclaves to which entry has only occasionally and grudgingly been allowed: the dream, the play, art, madness.

There is no metamorphosis without loss and without vision. People can only change form if they are willing to lose themselves, to wonder and imagine, to enter the undefined territories where the possible can be met with astonishment, yet without fear. The fairy tales for the inhabitants of a disenchanted world will no longer reproduce the phantasmic reality of the mythical lore, but they nevertheless still need to teach us to wonder.

4

The inner planet

Beyond an ecology of the symptom

Nan-in, a Japanese master of the Meiji era, received a visit from a university professor who had come to him to enquire about Zen. Nan-in served tea. He filled his guest's cup and then continued to pour. The professor watched his tea overflowing until he could contain himself no longer. 'The cup's full to the brim', he exclaimed, 'it can't take any more!' 'Like this cup', replied Nan-in, 'you're full to overflowing with your opinions and conjectures. How can I explain Zen to you unless you empty your cup?'

We treat the inner dimension of our experience like the professor in the parable. We believe that we know, that we already possess the required wisdom, that we are all experts on ourselves and have little left to learn. Introspection, we assume, requires no learning, and the expression of intimate feelings we leave to the poets, particularly now with the increasingly grave external problems competing for our attention. In recent years, the issue of nature has prominently captured the attention of the media and of the man in the street. In the form of the conservation and protection of our natural resources and the surrounding ecosystem, it has already established itself as the stock-in-trade of the political market and of the market *tout court*. But in the wake of the huge currency of the environmental issues (the ambivalence of which we nevertheless should not forget), the focus of our awareness of them has been restricted to the future of the planet as the physical-social habitat of the human species. It is the 'external planet' that preoccupies us behind the fears, appeals, and projects voiced by the environmentalists.

Yet there is another planet caught up in the radical process of transformation sweeping over us: the inner planet consisting of the biological, emotional, and cognitive structure that underlies the experience and relations of us all. We ought to concern ourselves with this inner planet as much as we do with the outer one, for the possibilities open to it and the dangers to which it is today submitted have reached critical dimensions from the point of view of both the life of the individual and the future of the species. Environmentalism seems to have overlooked this dimension and left it to the sidelines, paying only occasional and ritual homage to feminine difference or merely indulging in abstract intellectual debate. Even the belated discovery of the ecology of the mind, promptly transformed into a fad or a hasty maquillage on old clichés, has not led to any real development of a different point of view. Concern for the inner planet has in effect amounted to the mere addition of just another item to the already overcrowded agenda of problems demanding urgent attention; whereas, instead, it entails acceptance that we must change the way we look at things.

As with messages, or symptoms, from the body, we can adopt one of two attitudes towards ecological problems: we can 'solve' them or we can 'listen to' them. Technical, interventionist medicine has enshrined resolutive practice and ruled out 'listening'. The same attitude may prevail in our approach to ecological issues. The symptomatic nature of the phenomena is not recognized; instead, they are taken to constitute an exclusive province of action where success is measured in terms of efficiency of technique, forgetting that removing the symptom does not eliminate the illness but merely transfers it elsewhere.

Why has ecology become an issue? Not simply on account of the pollution obviously enough threatening our existence, with the environmental disaster visible on all sides; but also as a consequence of a profound change in our cultural and social perception of the reality in which we live. Unless we take account of this qualitative leap in the way the world is experienced through our minds and emotions, we may mistakenly restrict our concern solely to the environment. The ecological issue raises questions for contemporary consciousness that are far more radical than what has been disclosed in the dilemmas proclaimed by even the most extremist of the prophets of imminent biospheric doom.

The ecological issue is above all a *systemic problem*. That is to say, it reveals behind its surface the phenomenon of planetary interdependence and creates new frontiers of human consciousness and action. We have come to the end of linear causality, of monocausal explanation, of end-directed reasoning. We belong to systems where the circularity of causes calls for a restructuring of our cognitive patterns and of our expectations of reality. Above all, the present state of affairs requires us to abandon the sham of an objective outlook on the world. We must include in our field of observation the purposes, the affects, and the fragility of the observer:

everything that has always been considered to be subjective distortion and extraneous to the method of an authentically 'hard' science.

The confidence with which institutional science propounds its certainties is not supported by the reality of scientific inquiry, and it conflicts with the perceptions of a growing number of scientists. The limits of knowledge, the practical limitations of research undertakings, the wide margins of uncertainty characterizing scientific choices and decisions against the popular image of science as the assured pursuit of truth – these are all elements that should enter public discourse on the status of science. Such a questioning will undermine, perhaps even dismantle, the foundations of the faith in technology that takes science to be our only hope in averting catastrophe.

The ecological question also highlights the *cultural dimension* of human action. Industrial society organized its experience around the inevitability of economic laws and technical power. The ecological issue shows that the key to survival is no longer the system of means founded on purposive rationality. Our salvation lies in the system of ends, that is, in the cultural models which orient our behaviour. Culture – as the capacity to lend meaning to objects and relations – is the unbreachable confine within which questions concerning the destiny of humankind must be posed. It is impossible to imagine a livable future without acting as much on social relations, symbolic systems, and the circulation of information as on technical apparatuses. Those who seek to govern complexity by manipulating things are in danger of committing an error of perspective, of being trapped in a sort of substantive myopia. Today, effective action on things is increasingly dependent on an ability to alter the symbolic codes that organize daily life, political systems, and the patterns of production and consumption.

Our reality is a cultural construct, and our perceptions filter our relationships with the world. For the first time in the history of the species this statement is also true in a literal sense. In fact, our world today embraces the entire planet – a fact that has become possible owing to the power of information, of the cultural processes by which we represent the world. The consequences of this change are enormous. First and foremost among them is the increasing inability of the 'international' system founded on relations among sovereign nation states to deal with problems of global nature. But the emergence of a transnational dimension to issues and social actors is less a political question than a signal of the fact that mankind itself has come to culturally produce its sphere of action. The planet is no longer a physical place but has grown into a unified social space.

A further feature of the symptomatic function performed by the ecological question is that environmental problems affect *individuals qua individuals* and not as members of a group, a class, or a state. Although those memberships which in the modern age constituted the basis for the formation of interests and solidarity have not ceased to exist, it is increasingly evident that the future of the species and of the ecosystem is a problem that affects the lives of each and every one of us. Change can therefore no longer be dissociated from individual responsibility; direct and personal investment has become the condition and resource for intervention in the system.

Lastly, the ecological question signals that *conflict* is a physiological dimension of complex systems. The differentiation of interests and of cultures, and uncertainty as the constant condition of human action, give rise to an ineradicable quota of conflict in social life. Industrial culture considered conflict to emerge as the necessary outcome of exploitation or a social pathology. Recognizing that conflicts cannot be eliminated but only managed, negotiated, and resolved again entails the redefinition of the criteria of coexistence. Only an effort to make visible and negotiable the differences, possibilities, and constraints of communal human life, can lay the basis for new solidarity in both microrelations and macrosystems.

Lands of conquest

Granting that the ecological question signals these transformations, it is also necessary to accept the fact that we cannot address the problem of the planet without addressing the problem of ourselves. The ways in which we have historically constructed our relationships with the environment, with other species, and with nonindustrial cultures reflect the limits of our awareness, our inability to see and to hear, and the violence we have committed on that portion of ourselves to have resisted instrumental rationality. Concerning ourselves with the inner planet as an integral part of an ecological mentality means that we are called to go beyond an ecology of the symptom to assume responsibility for our being in the world. We must accept that we are that part of nature which can transform this same nature, because we can think of nature, imagine it, dream it. Hence we can also take care of it, beginning with the nature that lies within ourselves.

More than in any society of the past, our scientific knowledge and technology intervene in our natural environment and our biological structure. We have developed the reflexive capacity to produce knowledge about our actions and to give them symbolic representation over and above their specific content. The development of the cognitive sciences and of studies of the brain testifies to this increased intervention on ourselves as formal reflexivity, as pure symbolic capacity. In societies which depended much more closely on nature, human action was made manifest in its products.

Now that mankind's capacity for action on the natural and social environment has grown so great that we have acquired the power to actually destroy it, our capacity for action has become relatively independent of its products and is being transformed into a pure reflexive capacity which acts upon its own nature.

Thus, as well as from inhabiting our inner planet, we create it. The inner planet is not a natural datum, but nor is it a magical domain where dark forces operate. We take action to redraw its boundaries and map out its topography, we take possession of its territories like the oceanic explorers or modern conquistadors, poised to subject the new frontiers to the jurisdiction of rational control and to the transforming action of purposeful projects.

Today, new conflicts arise as we move in to appropriate this inner planet. On the one hand, we have learned how to participate in the formation of our identity, to take conscious action on ourselves, to explore and occupy the lands of our interior. On the other hand, we are denied this opportunity by the increasingly invasive intervention of the apparatuses of control and regulation, which with ever-advancing capacity aim to define the coordinates of the inner planet, set arbitrary borders, and lay claim to our motivations, affects, and our biological structure itself.

As today's individuals, we possess the ability and the option to consciously intervene in the production of our capacity for action; we can adjust our motivations, come into a closer contact with our bodies, work on our emotions. At the same time, however, we remain subject to processes of external manipulation which, in the name of techno-scientific rationality, colonize the inner planet and control the motivational, affective, and biological roots of our behaviour.

On the one hand, then, our potential for autonomous action, our reflexive ability to produce meaning and motivation for what we do, increases. We have available to us a potential for individuation – an opportunity to inhabit the territories of the inner planet as individuals; that is, to become individuals in the fullest possible sense – in the extent unknown to any previous epoch in the history of the human species. On the other hand, however, we are exposed to a parallel increase in the powers of control over the formation and transformation of our identities, to an erosion of the margins of our individual independence, and to an intensifying social regulation of our behaviour that tacitly forces us to manipulate our most intimate dimensions.

In education, in the definition of health and sickness, of normality and pathology, our need for autonomy comes into conflict with a standardizing rationality which uses scientific knowledge for intervention in motivational structure, for the pharmacological regulation of behaviour, for the ortho-pedic manipulation of interpersonal relationships that sets the standards of the 'correct' behaviour in having sex, raising children, making friends, forming couples, and so forth. Occupying ourselves with the inner planet therefore also directs our attention to the ways in which it may become a land of conquest and a tutelage of external authority.

The deterministic patterns we inherited from positivism have dissipated, with other conceptions of the relationship between biological life, mental experience, and social reality assuming their place. The impressive growth of the neurosciences over the last twenty-five years has brought along with it the development of entirely new insights into what it is to be human. Holistic models have been constructed which are at odds with the reduc-tionist tradition of modern science and which affirm the impossibility of separating microcosm and macrocosm. The inner planet is no longer an essence, but an articulation of levels and systems which alters the way we perceive ourselves.

A 'female' route to the interior has opened up which has triggered our sensitivity to forgotten levels of experience. The scientific model metaphor of the hemispheric specialization (the rational faculties on the left side, the intu-itive ones on the right) has provided a very popular representation of our mental life. Beyond its scientific interest, the metaphor of the 'right brain' has forcefully restated our awareness of the fact that logical-rational thought, the calculation of means and ends, does not exhaust human experience, and that the dimensions of intuition, feeling, and an immediate and global relation-ship with reality are equally important constituents of our being.

Finally, the dualistic heritage of the mind–body relationship has been called into question, and we have begun to leave the dominant model of linear causality behind. The body as a relational vehicle also expresses our inner nature and translates the programme drawn up by our biological structure into behaviour. The body, however, is not a machine commanded by the mind; rather, it 'embodies' the mind and enables us to exist as unified wholes.

In safeguarding and developing the inner planet we have to prepare to fight against its colonizers and we can incorporate this enormous wealth of knowledge into our field of experience. We must learn to explore, to settle, and to cultivate rather than passively submit.

New maps of the planet Man

What we have learned about the human brain over the last twenty-five years far outstrips all the knowledge accumulated in previous history. The development of research into the brain and into the relationships between biology and behaviour has opened up limitless fields for scientific enquiry. In this, a new branch of knowledge has been created whose discoveries oblige us to redefine the conventional boundaries drawn between the scientific disciplines. Neuroscience is today an enormous, bustling, constantly expanding laboratory where the new maps of the inner planet are being drawn.

This field of study, with its extraordinary dynamism and frenetic activity, raises the most emotive of scientific questions: how does the human brain know itself? Put differently, what do we know of our knowledge, how do we learn to learn, how can we investigate our memory, emotions, and behaviour through the activity of the mind which at the same time is the very object of its own analytical operations?

The field of the neurosciences is vast and ramified. One recent 'encyclopedia' on the subject comprises over 700 entries written by more than 600 specialists. However, the impression one gains is that of a provisional balance-sheet itemizing of a field whose borders have yet to be specified. To inquire into the brain – as the 'instrument' or 'organ' of the human mind – is to roam among a variety of topics ranging from neurotransmitters (the elements which circulate information among the neurons) to the evolution of language, to memory, to the mechanisms of pain control; from artificial intelligence to perception, from learning to the effects of pharmaceuticals, to the development of the nervous system, to the psychosomatic dimensions of the brain.

The field of the neurosciences is conspicuous not only for its magnitude and rapid growth; it is an area of controversy where often conflicting theories and models compete. Its creative fervour is fed by intense and sometimes acrimonious debate. Depending on one's ethical or social point of view, the developments and applications of pharmacology and neurosurgery open up exciting or disquieting horizons. Suffice it to mention the modern medicine, with the help of which, since the identification of certain neurotransmitters, it is now possible to successfully intervene in highly specific sectors of behaviour and the emotions. Similarly, we may note here the no longer science-fiction possibility of implanting 'young nerve cells in old brains', as one of the most celebrated neurosurgeons has put it.

But even before such applications, controversy has begun to centre on the models being constructed as discoveries accumulate. What is today known of the intensity of cerebral activity surprises even the researchers themselves. The brain is a concentration of energies, an enormous accumulator burning massive amounts of sugar and performing operations of an almost indescribable complexity. One need only think of the instantaneous collaboration between memory, emotions, senses, and muscles that makes the miracle of human verbal communication possible. This enormous complexity calls into question the mechanistic model of evolution, and forces us into a new conception of the mind as a continuous fluctuation, a constant reorganization of the inner structures of the brain.

The multiple and articulated structure of the brain is one of the nodes around which current debate over the different models of the mind concentrates. The different functions of the right and left hemispheres of the brain, or its 'vertical' specialization (reptilian brain, the limbic system, the neocortex) have been made widely known to the general public through the media. But behind this popularization lies serious research into cerebral dissociation (split brain) and multiple personality disorders, and the arguments over the first results obtained by this research. The debate seems to indicate that the simplified model of brain hemisphere specialization has been superseded, its place being taken by a theory envisaging a 'confederation' of cerebral systems, a network of intercommunication 'modules'. In the more circumscribed field of the differences between right and left brain, attention has shifted to the mediating function of the intermediate area between the two hemispheres, the *corpus callosum*, which is the principal control centre for communications within the neocortex.

Fascinating hypotheses have been put forward as simple preliminary models have been developed, and collaboration has intensified between the neurobiologists, psychologists, and social scientists investigating cognitive processes and their relation to behaviour: how are perception, attention, memory, and emotions, the essential components of our cognitive experience, linked together?

Another crucial area of study concerns the relation between neurology and the psycho-social dimensions of illness. Neuroscientific research clearly shows that purely biological filters protecting our body (for example, the immune system), alone, provide inadequate resistance against the attack of the typical diseases of our time – such as cardiovascular diseases, immune deficiencies, cancer, mental illness. The brain, with its complex capacity to intervene in our cognitive and emotional experiences, is the go-between that links the social and psychological dimensions of modern illness with the biological filters which defend the organism. The brain in this sense is a key to health.

The importance and the role of cognitive and emotional variables in biological defence and healing have been most clearly demonstrated by research into the placebo effect. Furthermore, studies of biofeedback and the voluntary influence exercised by yogis over their neurovegetative systems also provide examples of the power of the 'mind' over the nervous, circulatory, and immune systems, thereby demonstrating how much the influence of 'thought' on our bodies has been neglected.

The placebo effect, in fact, promises to develop into the most fertile field of investigation into the relation between brain and health. Previously considered to be merely an effect of autosuggestion, this phenomenon is increasingly attracting the attention of researchers as an example of the human organism's 'mental' capacity to heal itself. By 'placebo effect' is meant every response attributable to a therapeutic substance or procedure but not connected with the pharmacological or other specific properties of the treatment. Western medicine is based on the analysis of physiological aspects in both the onset of the disease and in its cure. The fact that a pharmacologically inert substance can change the state of the organism is a rather striking anomaly.

Research into the placebo effect is conducted along both biological and psycho-social lines. In the biological approach, a connection has been established between the placebo and the release of endorphins, the natural painkillers secreted by the body. The psycho-social explanation has discarded the banal hypothesis of self-suggestion and addresses personality variables, the doctor–patient relationship, and expectations based on previous experiences. Common to these two approaches is their stress on the role of the brain as the mediator between cognitive and emotional experiences on the one hand, and the biochemical dimensions of the nervous system on the other.

What is going on in neurosciences is not merely a series of debates among specialists. The research, controversies, and critical issues in the field map out new routes for exploration of our inner planet and at the same time spell out the risks of colonization. Research into the brain opens up new horizons for analysis of the mind and redraws the boundaries between mind and body. It confronts us, that is, with a new conception of our self and compels us to leave the dualistic universe behind.

Mindbody/bodymind

The paradox of language is that while we search for a new unity between mind and body, we are still imprisoned by two terms bequeathed to us by the past. Meanwhile, research has pushed much further ahead in its identification of the communication links between mind and body, which now figure as the two poles of a circular relationship. Yet also science encounters the same difficulty in finding the language to express its new discoveries. In 1964, George Salomon at the University of California in Los

Angeles coined the term 'psychoimmunology' to describe the interaction between mental activity and the body's immune system. Since then, the term, and the field of research that it designates, have been enriched with further refinements and adjustments which represent not solely nuances of meaning. 'Psychoneuroimmunology' seems today to be the most widely used term, although Salomon himself often resorts to 'psycho-social neuroimmunology' and other writers prefer such terms as 'neuroimmunomodulation' and 'behavioural immunology'. As always happens when a new area of research is being explored, the debate on terminology reflects epistemological premises and theoretical models, as well as ethical and political beliefs which often come into conflict.

Whatever the case may be, there is no doubt that an entirely new field of study is being created by research into the relationships between brain, mental activity, and immune system. These relationships are sometimes difficult to disentangle from socio-environmental and behavioural variables. Hence the difficulty of marking out the territory, finding a language to define it, and building consensus in the scientific community on how to describe it.

Since the first reports by Salomon and his coworkers on their discoveries in 1969, a large quantity of empirical evidence and experimental data has been pouring forth which confirms a close link between the central nervous system and the immune system. Defence of the body is apparently inseparable from the mental and affective life of the individual. The first laboratory discoveries showed that stress suppresses responses of the immune systems and that, vice versa, an early ability to cope with stress may strengthen these responses.

The considerable amount of observation and research accumulated over the last twenty years seems to indicate the definite existence of a network of communication between the brain and the immune system. The items of evidence on which reasonable consensus exists remain parts of a mosaic as yet incomplete but nevertheless significant. There is, first of all, a correlation between certain personality traits and a tendency for immune defences to be suppressed. Reversely, mental health seems to correlate with high indices of defensive potential in the body (as, for example, the number of cells which function as 'natural killers'). Moments of crisis or of existential tension (bereavement, separation) reduce the immune response, as do mental disorders or serious emotional disturbances. Stressful experiences at an early age have immunological consequences, and researchers are beginning to describe the processes by which shocks influence the body's system of immunity. By contrast, an increase in nerve cell activity can be detected when the immune system is activated. Research into neurotransmitters confirms that the central nervous system and the immune system are regulated by substances with similar biochemical properties. Finally, it has been demonstrated that acting on a person's emotional life and behaviour, for example through the application of psychotherapy, relaxation techniques, or biofeedback, strengthens the body's immune response. Research into AIDS, now a greatly expanding field, also shows that the patients who survive the longest are those best able to generate a positive emotional response. These patients are people who have already had to cope with suffering in their lives, who are strongly committed to the future, and who can use even illness to give a new meaning to their existence.

Some of these results apparently confirm what common sense has always maintained, and which the medical wisdom of antiquity, from Hippocrates to Galen, bequeathed to technological culture. The communication network between mind and body which enables the organism to react to pathogenic agents or stress has now been more accurately described. It may therefore soon be possible consciously to intervene to improve personal balance and health. Interpretation of research data, however, is still a matter of controversy, and specialist debate has not yet reached any firm conclusions: the weight of behavioural or environmental factors, and the role of emotional dimensions or genetic factors, are questions which can be answered in a variety of ways.

If anything, however, the controversial terrain of psycho-neuro-immunology seems to preclude any continued possibility of employing models of linear causality. Circular models or networks certainly furnish a better interpretation of the complex relationships between mind and body; they emerge as a communication network in which more than one language is spoken.

As the barren flatlands of dualism and debate on purely philosophical premises have been left behind, the problem of the mind–body relation has been framed from an entirely new perspective. The perception of the connections between brain, immune system, and emotional states has been fundamentally altered, before all by the results from the research into neurotransmitters. Of particular relevance here are recent discoveries by research into neuropeptides. As simple substances, present in the body in relatively small numbers, neuropeptides are chemical messengers which perform an extremely complex but still largely unexplored function. These signal molecules, or communication molecules, seem neurologically more significant than the synapses, the connections among nerve cells which until only recently were regarded as the main transmitters of chemical messages.

The neuropeptides link together the nervous system, the endocrine system, and the immune system in a bidirectional information network. They are able to receive and transmit information, apart from controlling the flow of that information through feedback mechanisms. The substances that control moods and emotional states are therefore the same that control the body's defence systems. Like the nervous system, the immune system is also capable of cognition and communication. The neuropeptides govern the cells of the immune system as they perform their task of defending the organism. The neuropeptide receptors, strategically placed in various parts of the body, including the limbic zone of the brain, create a tightly woven network of high sensitivity.

These chemical transmitters are associated with a wide range of psychophysical states, moods, and emotional responses: pleasure, pain, learning, appetite, sexuality, anxiety. They therefore constantly intervene in the perception or alteration of consciousness. Emotions thus lie not only in the mind, but in the body as well. The capacity for conscious perception seems at this point to spread throughout the body, and comprehensively redefines the traditional account of the mind-body relationship. It becomes impossible to think of the mind as a function which exercises itself *on* the body. The signal molecules provide us with the key to an understanding of the vital energy that circulates in the body, and of our physical reality as an animate space and a network of messages imbued with emotional and cognitive connotations.

To explore and protect

Our discourse on the inner planet, however, does not concern scientific language alone. The experience of each one of us, our conscious scrutiny of our own selves, are precious and inexhaustible sources of knowledge. We must grant them equal dignity of status and use them to mark out our progress into the future. The lands of the inner planet are limitless and we have only just begun to explore them; the next few years seem destined to reveal further unknown continents. And even at this moment of the exploration, coarse and avaricious *hidalgos* are equipping themselves to set off in search of the new El Dorado. It should, however, be possible for every one of us to become both an explorer and a custodian of these lands, so unique and so intimately part of us. Taking charge of them, protecting them against the dangers that threaten, cultivating them with respect and without violence, are duties which we are already called upon to fulfil. It is a task which involves each and every one of us, but which we nevertheless cannot treat as an individual problem.

An ecology of economic, political, and technological choices cannot operate independently of an ecology of the everyday, of the words and gestures with which we call into being or annihilate the inner planet. To pay attention and respect to the details; to be aware that we are part of a whole and we need to connect the different elements into this whole; to value the path and not only the end; to acknowledge polarities and the limitation of each pole – all these are attitudes promoting in the everyday a different relation between the inner planet and its natural and social environment. The various forms of reflexivity and communication in which we engage form a terrain which calls for a new and qualitatively different level of learning, a kind of learning which is already beginning to supplant a culture exclusively centred on contents, values, and goals. In the age when the high pace of change produces increasingly rapid obsolescence accompanied by the constant replacement of contents, the forms and processes of human action rise to a crucial importance. The 'how' of action attains an importance equal to the 'what', if not even greater.

The emergence of corporeal, cognitive, and relational processes as a field of deliberate intervention signifies the transformation of behaviour into messages, into meaningful discourse – that is, into a discourse capable of conveying the deep-lying link between the within and the without, between the nature that we are and the nature that we inhabit. The challenge that lies before us is to exist in the continuity and discontinuity that ties nature and culture together; in the paradox of becoming consciously – that is, culturally – nature. *Homo sapiens*, the erect and cerebralized species, must undertake the task of recognizing itself as standing 'between earth and sky', as ancient oriental wisdom would put it. We must accept our rootedness in the soil on which we stand, and affirm our aspiration to the sky above our head. The inner planet, the point where body and language meet between behaviour and reflexivity, is the connection, the conjunction between earth and sky.

As stated, we are only now beginning to explore the most accessible frontiers of our inner landscape. Not every discovery will belong to the order of rationality as the modern West has come to define it – often to the frustration of our deepest spiritual needs. New mysticisms are being born today as a testimony to an unsatisfied thirst for the sacred, with, moreover, all the violence that follows the footsteps of every preacher of salvation. The conquistador counts on the force of arms; the missionary arriving at his wake swears by the violence of the word. The task of colonizing the inner planet may yet be divided between the two.

Confronting these very real dangers requires that we follow the paradoxical path of desacralizing the sacred, by being open to that which constantly evades us, by suspending the word, by being present and waiting – in other words, by keeping our cup empty so that it can be filled. The difficulties involved in such a radical change of perspective, however, remain as considerable as their overcoming is critical; even the attempt at addressing it stumbles on the existing vocabulary too threadbare for the purpose. Yet it is precisely to this quest that the inner planet calls those who have passed through the process of disenchantment and dare to wonder.

5

Body as limit, body as message

Body to body

The body invades our everyday experience. It has triumphed in the public and private arenas, as is evident in the profusion of images and objects that display it, and in the reception of the messages and appeals that make it their subject. Services providing care for the body proliferate, and experts are now to be found to cater to our every bodily need. Interest in physical health is in the increase, gymnastics has assumed expressive and hyper-technological forms, oriental disciplines and yoga enjoy unprecedented popularity. Although this search seems to concern single individuals only, it in fact expresses a transformation of needs which has led us to search, inspect, touch, name the body.

The body has acquired a new meaning first and foremost as a consequence of the way that we now define ourselves. We spring from a culture where the corporeal dimensions of human experience were either ignored or treated merely as instrumental to physical performance or work, always subordinate to mental and spiritual activities of a higher order. Today we have discovered our natural dimension; we have come to realize that we belong to nature, that we are but one species amongst the others. Under the influence of a divine principle of transcendence, the body was nothing but an index of the fallen, degraded nature which hampered the free rein of the spirit. Otherwise, relative to the great destinies towards which history was seen as moving, the body could never be anything more than an instrument. Now, however, as the gods have indisputably and finally left the stage and history no longer can promise any insured outcome as its conclusion, we are prepared to comprehend the nature that is ourselves. The renewed interest in the body expresses this new awareness of our belongingness to nature and of the fact that it is in nature that our roots and dignity lie.

Another factor which affirms our focus on the body and on its enhancement is the dimension of desire. The culture that we come from was suspicious of anything that had to do with the level of instincts, urges, or deep-seated needs. In its religious version of spirit possession and of sin, or in its secular-puritan version of bourgeois morality, the principle persisted that the impulses of the body were fundamentally evil in their origin and influence, and thus to be considered injurious to proper conduct of life if not adequately contained. Today, there is a growing awareness that the body expresses a vital energy which brings us into contact with reality and with others, an energy which enables us to create and to transform reality.

There has, then, been a radical change in our attitude to the dimension of desire. The word 'desire' has now entered everyday discourse and tends to be gradually replacing words with traditionally pejorative connotations such as 'instinct' or 'urge'. Similarly, the term 'energy' is now part of our commonplace lexicon, being used to indicate the dimension of bodily experience which, through the pressure of nature, brings us into contact with nature so that we may transform it.

The culture of the body, furthermore, has led to the concrete discovery of the condition that we, as individuals, stand as such only in relation to others. As a symbol and instrument of communication, the body acts as the channel for our affectivity. Interpersonal relationships are not constituted solely by sentiments and ideas; they also involve a physical encounter between bodies. This awareness was always very profound in traditional cultures, where the body performed a vital role not only in the relationships between the sexes but in all the circumstances of social life. The modern West has progressively eliminated the body from interpersonal relations, which it has transformed into neutralized and aseptic role relationships and deprived as far as possible of any reference to the cumbersome and importunate body.

We are now laboriously rediscovering that the relationship between human beings also involves the body. Sexuality is no longer consigned to the dark realm of the instincts, but is taken to be a profoundly human form of communication, a relational instrument that introduces us to love. Passion loses its negative meaning and becomes synonymous with feeling rooted in the body. Emotions regain their earthy consistency, fed as they are by moods and sounds, by odours and vibrations. Fear and joy, tenderness and sorrow are not merely ideas but tears and laughter, warmth and trembling. The encounter between humans becomes once again an encounter between bodies and between words.

The body is, finally, for each of us the personal realm, the field of that specific awareness which distinguishes us from others. The return to the body fuels our search for identity; our body is the secret place for which only we possess the key of access and where we may return to confirm our experience that we exist as individuals. The body is our unique and unalienable possession which gives us the power of self-recognition in an age when other forms of identification break down. No one else can tell us what we feel within our bodies; only we can express ourselves through the body.

Discourse and practice concerning the body thus evince our need to affirm that we belong to nature, our search for a channel through which we may express the energy of desire and communicate with others, and our need to give an underpinning to our existence as individuals. But the 'body boom' no less signifies its concomitant and already completed reduction to a market phenomenon. As an attractively packaged commodity or as a symbolically loaded message, the body generates business for important sectors of the economy, from cosmetics to fashion, from the erotic press to pharmaceutical products. We are submerged in the flow of images of a body pressed into service to sell practically everything. In that function, pleasure arises to a paramount position: we are inundated by sex manuals, guides to good health, recipes for the better use of a body devoid of its charge of eros and desire. Simultaneously, however, the body acts as the focus for our needs for freedom, expression, and creativity.

Whenever we talk about the body, whenever we use it, we move across an ambivalent terrain. For we are dealing with the body that constitutes both a 'subject' and an 'object': with a body that is ourselves and with a body that is submitted to an ever-intensifying and ever-broadening outside intervention. All the fundamental events of our existence – events in which the body is by definition involved – are in contemporary society regulated by the criteria of normality imposed by doctors, expert opinion, and models of consumption: birth and death, sexuality and love, reproduction and the education of our children, health and sickness, clothing and body care are today regarded through the heteronomous definitions issued by the authority backed by diagnostic precision and an unlimited supply of services.

This is a paradoxical situation, for the body of which we speak, the body to which messages, advice, and prescriptions are addressed, is *our* body. It is *we ourselves*: the foundation of our persona and the locus of every energy, of every possibility for action. As such, this body may be expropriated from us only upon our own consent. We know its weight and lightness, its suffering and pleasure; it is still to our bodies that we turn as we seek to summon up force to resist external pressure, to steer our energies in the direction that we feel corresponds to our needs, to affirm that we are distinct individuals.

Discourse on the body is profoundly marked by this ambivalence. The cultures of the body are either swiftly transformed into rhetoric or new mysticism, or they are exploited for the market. The rhetoric of the body and its marketing as a commodity disguise its ambivalence or dissolve it through overexposure. Yet taking cognizance of the body in our everyday life fosters awareness of ongoing change; it brings to light neglected or unknown levels of experience. Paying attention to the body is therefore essential, but it also constitutes a provisional stage along the road to awareness, one point of view that may reveal another and bring hidden questions to the surface. The body is a message to be listened to, to be deciphered, to be answered. The body speaks, and not only through its public display, but personally to each one of us through its signals. In that, it may also be listened point out ways to respond, as ways to responsibility. We can answer for our bodies because we have learned to answer to them.

Minor ailments

One of the commonest ways in which the body impinges on our everyday lives is through minor illness, all those small complaints and physical disorders which do not normally require the attentions of a doctor, provided they do not turn chronic, more serious, or give rise to further, more impairing symptoms. All of us are afflicted to a varying extent by minor ailments. As a commonplace topic of everyday conversation we talk about them all the time. Yet, in fact, we never take them seriously, for they represent a frame or boundary of our experience which we do not feel is worth bothering about.

What is the significance to us of these physical states and bodily sensations that so constantly affect us? The experience of such minor ailments is an experience of the everyday; nothing exceptional, nothing strange. Illness is repetitive and in a certain sense banal; it has a lot to do with habit. Illness therefore has all the features of routine, and this is precisely why we treat it as normal. However, unlike the other commonplace experiences of daily life, our minor disorders contain a specific feature, an alarming and threatening element.

It is not so much the annoyance our minor ailments cause that bothers us. Obviously we do feel unwell, sometimes we suffer pain or irritation, but in this our illnesses resemble those numerous other events of everyday life that distress or trouble us. What distinguishes minor illnesses from other common experiences, however, is precisely the element of menace they contain. On the one hand, our ailments belong to the scenario of the usual, and this is partly why we treat them as commonplace and neglect them, living free of concern with illness in the routine of everyday times and gestures. On the other hand, however, our minor disorders preoccupy us; we cannot ignore them, they hover over our daily lives, they mark it and they colour it.

Although minor ailments are physical, they merge in one with our psychological experience, with our states of mind and emotions. The distinctive feature of our minor ailments is the fact that they belong to the body: we suffer from stomachache, headache, backache, and the like. Our ailments also link to a temporal dimension: for some of us they last for a day, for others a season, for others still they depend on meteorological time. Thus there is always a temporal connotation to our illnesses; there is a chronology and a cycle they follow. Time is a vitally important dimension which characterizes the enormous individual variability of these experiences.

Another obvious but nevertheless significant dimension to our ailments is their relation to space. They vary according to certain spatial and geographical characteristics. For example, they relate more closely to some places rather than others, they depend on whether we move or stay still. Finally, our minor ailments are normally affected by our relationships. It is common knowledge that a person's health varies radically according to her/his affective situation. As we move through a typical day we may pass from a general feeling of well-being to a headache caused by a disagreeable encounter. Or, vice versa, we may enter a situation fraught with tension and pain, and leave it buoyed up by the sympathy, the enthusiasm, the joy that it has evoked in us. Each of us could plot a map of our minor ailments along these dimensions; a spatio-temporal map and a relational map of the body's minor afflictions.

Our minor ailments almost never correlate with major events, with the great changes in our lives: separations, bereavements, job changes, emotional upheavals. These occasions are marked by more severe or more intense signals, of great physical well-being or of great suffering. Minor ailments are as opaque as everyday life, and they reflect its features of normality and repetition. They are ubiquitous to the degree that we appear never to bother about them, although in fact we are constantly occupied with them, in the same way as we clean our teeth or look at ourselves in the mirror. Minor ailments are our boring, faithful companions, our constant partners as we move through daily life.

In a cultural context which stresses change and efficiency, which constantly urges us to choose, to make decisions, to cope with different situations, these minor afflictions, these daily companions of ours, have become an absolute nuisance. They are as annoying as unwelcome guests arriving for a visit at the weekend and then staying on until Monday, at a time when we are extremely busy but still obliged to reluctantly look after them. The commonest cultural remedy for minor ailments is to treat them as guests who outstayed their welcome: we ignore them or pretend that they have already left. Our normal attitude is therefore to forget that this part of our experience exists.

There is an analogy here with a more general attitude towards all the routine dimensions of everyday life. Our culture preaches that household appliances – those omnipresent gadgets we use to cope with the boredom of repetition – can free us from the tedium of our daily chores. Yet we know that this is a false promise, that as we load the washing machine and operate the blender we are once again trapped by routine. What counts, however, is the importance assigned to variability, to the possibility of being ever new, and to the attempt to eliminate repetition.

If there is thus a cultural tendency to deny and cover up the repetitive dimension of experience, our minor ailments are an anomaly. We can successfully alleviate or eliminate other routine aspects of our daily lives by multiplying, albeit fictitiously, their variable aspects. We can inject novelty into many areas of our experience: new holidays, new friends, a new television programme can at least feed to the illusion that we have defeated boredom. But there is a specific feature of our minor ailments, however much we seek to systematically ignore them in our daily routines, which we find difficult to eliminate: the element of menace contained in them.

Unlike those other aspects of routine which are purely habit, our experience of minor illness contains a danger and an alarm: the fear or the possibility of serious disease. This area of experience conceals a dark nucleus, a menacing time bomb ticking away in the background: ordinary ailments may lead to major illnesses. They are therefore the harbingers, the signals of potentially more severe suffering, the first steps towards Disease with a capital D.

The other aspects of our daily lives are only boring, they weigh us down with their monotonous repetition; in the case of illness, however, the repetition becomes the cyclical, even daily, reappearance of a looming menace. Thus the cultural process I described above is flanked by the psychological process by which we keep the threat at bay and by which we gloss over the peril that constantly resurfaces in our daily lives and reminds us of the harrowing illnesses that may lie in store. This creates a sort of alliance between a psychological need which compels us to keep the threat at arm's length, and a cultural tendency which emphasizes variability, innovation, and efficiency and which induces us to shrug off our minor ailments, which in addition to being tedious and repetitive also reduce our performance ability.

The silence of the body

How, then, do we normally respond to our minor ailments? As I already noted, the most ordinary reaction consists in ignoring them by mentally purging our bodies of the presence of these annoying 'guests'. This, however, does not mean that we are no longer physically aware of the complaints that afflict us; only we make no room in our mental (cognitive and affective) framework for naming, for giving a meaning to, this particular part of our experience. Often we no longer say 'I've got a headache' or 'I've got a pain in the stomach', but instead take refuge in the more generic 'I feel ill', which supplies an interesting way of avoiding the definition – that is, the localization and delimitation – of experience.

The other common response to a minor ailment is to resort to the trusted care of the medicine. In modern society, the consumption of painkillers, tranquillizers, sedatives, and stimulants has reached astounding levels, accounting for the largest portion of the pharmaceutical industry's market share. Pharmaceuticals are used for two purposes. First, they have the physiological effect of reducing or eliminating distress, of physically ousting the unwelcome guest. Secondly, from the psychological point of view, pharmaceuticals also, and more importantly, erase the existence of the ailment from our minds. Where previously there was a presence, we create, mentally and affectively, an empty space. This is the most important effect of the pharmaceuticals, and it explains their massive, indiscriminate, and uncontrolled use. Although their efficiency as temporary painkillers may not be called into question from a physiological point of view, the chief purpose of medication is precisely to act psychologically as magic philtres. Their main function is to erase the presence of the unwanted guest; in other words, they reduce or annul the menace of the serious disease of which that visitor reminds us by its presence.

Such a practice has by now spread systematically to involve even those minor ailments that have always affected half of the humankind. Here I refer to the menstrual cycle and to the minor disorders associated with it: cramps, physical changes, alterations of mood, and other such effects. Today, there is also general recognition of premenstrual tension as a physical syndrome, and a specific medical practice has been developed for its treatment. Female emancipation and the entry of certain categories of women into occupational life have been accompanied by an obligation for them to fulfil a variety of new roles, and thereby to also minimize the practical impediments created by the menstrual cycle. The minor ailments associated with menstruation and the disorders by now identified as constituting a genuine syndrome are subjected to massive pharmacological intervention. This medicalization is directed not only at the physiological datum of the cycle, but also at all the varieties of behaviour and psycho-physical states that it gives rise to. The physical and behavioural signals, the moods and the affective states connected with the menstrual cycle, today effectively constitute a pathology.

The silence of the body thus represents the everyday counterpoint to its inordinate display in public. While body-related images and signs assail us from all directions, the only body that counts – ours – is consigned to silence.

The body of the word

This said, our minor ailments continue to stand as a presence in our daily lives that must be given a meaning. In the diagnosis given in Genesis, divine displeasure inflicts sickness and pain, in its minor and major versions, as the price we must pay for expiation. Today, however, this universe of meaning is entirely unable to sustain our experience. We need new mean-ings to come to terms with pain, including the everyday and trifling pain of the body. Our minor disorders serve as a signal of our finitude. The premonition of terminal disease is none other than a reminder or an admonition that the most profound experience of our life is the knowledge that we are mortal. It is as if every slight headache or twinge of indigestion contains a molecule of this fundamental memory; as if every minor ailment brings a particle of meaning into our everyday lives which we are called upon to acknowledge. Whether we erase this presence by mental elabora-tion or through the effect of pharmaceuticals, or whether we assume the responsibility of giving meaning to our finiteness, remains entirely our own decision.

This provides the basis for a redefinition of the relationship between minor and major illness. At issue here is not just the menace that I discussed above, but a fundamental law of our physiological makeup. Minor dis-orders are also symptoms, they transmit signals to us. To assume the task of investing this experience with meaning signifies not only living with finiteness, but reading the body's signs as messages.

Minor ailments are not the announcement of the extreme catastrophe – for this we already possess a bestiary well-stocked with monsters. Rather, they signal an imbalance, a neglected need which chooses to express itself through the body: a change in the environment that has not been acknowl-edged, an excess or a lack of energy applied to a task, a disequilibrium in personal rhythms. The pain of the body is thus not solely a threat; it is also an appeal, a summons which must be answered.

In the foregoing, I have addressed minor ailments as irksome companions, as inconveniences, as unwelcome guests. Equally, however, they could be regarded as our friends. There are three reasons for this. First, and most generally, they constantly remind us of our finiteness and force us into awareness of the fact. Secondly, they signal an imbalance to which the body is already reacting by giving us pain; they invite us to consciously respond to the signal instead of ignoring it. Serious illness is always the culmination of a repetitive series of signals which have either gone unheeded or which have been silenced with the force of pharmaceuticals. If the signal is stifled, the problem proclaimed by the signal is also reduced to silence. Thirdly, if minor ailments constitute a sign of our capacity for adaptation and response, they not only remind us that we are finite and shall die, but also that we are immersed in life, that we translate an existential, environmental, and relational condition into our bodies. This minute and quotidian presence of the signals emitted by our bodies expresses an enormous potential for life and great dynamism. The body's signals are the ineluctable clock of existence which tells us that we are alive but finite, finite but alive.

The way we live the same experience changes significantly according to whether we can confer meaning to our minor ailments or will, instead, react to them by mechanically and indiscriminately submitting to the ready cure of the pharmaceutical products. Usually, to be sure, we oscillate between the two extremes: either we belittle the significance of the signals or we exaggerate their threat. If we are able to enter into dialogue with the signals of the body, they become transformed into messengers of health prompting conscious responses. Any sensory experience of physical discomfort will alter when we view it from a perspective that can render it meaningful. Changing the cultural and mental framework we apply to the body's signals also transforms their perceptive connotation, with all the consequences we now know possible to flow from such an altered state. The physical perception of a painful sensation changes profoundly according to whether we try to ignore it, treat it as a menacing symptom of possible disease, or accept to feel it as a signal to be listened to and responded to.

Events of the body

Our everyday relationship with the body's messages also constitutes a pedagogy of existence. In our relations with minor ailments and, more generally, with the signals transmitted by our bodies, we may learn to see the great events of the body – birth, sickness, and death – in a new light.

In complex societies birth is no longer inevitable. Contraception on the one hand, and techniques for intervention in pregnancy and childbirth on the other, have radically altered a phenomenon that conditioned societies for thousands of years: throughout millennia, the reproduction of the social system depended primarily on its biological base and on the fertility of the population. The birth rate varied according to environmental conditions and genetic and evolutionary factors; but this remained a quasi-natural datum that was almost entirely immune to human intervention.

Deliberate birth control – in the sense of interference in the very possibility of childbirth and its circumstances – has profoundly altered this apparently immutable biological premise, which has now been rendered a field of choice and decision-making. This, of course, does not apply to all the inhabitants of the world, but the seed of the change is present and potentially generalizable. When and how to give birth is no longer a matter of destiny but of choice. Our life-giving bodies, especially our female bodies, which bear life and bring it into the world, are no longer the blind vehicles of a biological necessity: they have become an arena of possibility, deliberate attention, and choice. Nevertheless, they can also, and at the same time, become objects delivered into the hands of an external, technical and medical, power, which turns them once again into simple vessels, whose content can only be investigated by specialists. In their potential to give life, our bodies are then at stake as never before.

At the opposite pole, death, too, is no longer a necessity of nature and has now been transformed much more overtly into a cultural fact. We are increasingly able both to avert death and to intervene in its timing and circumstances. The average age of the population increases, while ever more sophisticated biomedical techniques are employed to prolong life still. Death, by the same token, has become something to be removed from the social environment; it becomes confined to specialized institutions and administered by the 'men in the white coats' – the apostles of the aseptic rationality of the health care apparatus. Today, most of us die in a hospital. For traditional societies, death was a natural datum which could not be contradicted, a destiny to be feared and exorcised. For precisely this reason, it was cultivated by ritual and converted from an alien force into a familiar one. In our culture, death instead undergoes thorough socialization, becoming thereby neutralized and woven into technical, medical, and pharmacological circuits seemingly intent on eliminating the personal experience of death. We are born as individuals and as individuals we die altogether. The final act of our bodies belongs as much to us as life itself. Communal rites need to be replaced today by a new capacity to situate death in a meaningful connection. An extraneous body, a body machine, will only leave us bewildered when it ceases to function. An inhabited body, on the other hand, an old friend, can teach us how to take our leave of it.

And the moment of leave-taking may actually become the culmination of our closeness.

Tied to birth and death, as the unique events of the body, is the experience of illness – an event that may repeat itself but which leaves the imprint of extraordinary forces in the histories of our bodies. Affluent societies have freed themselves from the scourge of disease as a collective catastrophe. The great epidemics of the past have dwindled or disappeared, the impact of infectious diseases and causes of infant mortality has been dramatically blunted (even if at the world scale tremendous imbalances still exist). However, their place has been taken by new forms of socially related pathology: stress, cancer, AIDS, pollution-related diseases, iatrogenic illnesses induced by the indiscriminate consumption of pharmaceuticals. Our everyday imaginations are haunted by the menacing spectres of new monsters bred by our social life itself.

This dramatic paradox is flanked by a second. The general improvement in sanitary, dietary, and housing conditions, along with the spread of health education and information, have heightened our ability to perceive our state of health. Therewith our autonomy in taking care of our own well-being, and our responsibility for it, has correspondingly increased. In parallel, however, the health care system has extended its range of operational efficiency, issuing a precise and external definition of pathology and health. This definition promotes the rise of care or health management technology and apparatuses connected to welfare policies. Preventive measures are now being applied to entire social categories with no regard for individual differences. The definition of illness and its prevention shift towards infancy and towards neonatal and intrauterine life.

If we happen to belong to a category officially at risk, to a section of the population singled out by administrative fiat, we may be declared ill by decree and consequently subjected to health treatment by authorized instance dedicated for the particular therapeutic function. In childcare, in the definition of mental health, in pregnancy and childbirth, in sexology, we are already subjected to intervention which defines us as healthy or ill according to criteria entirely extraneous to the real events of our bodies. Setting health standards independent from the individual feelings is a necessity for welfare policies which are in principle addressed to the totality of citizens. In any case, they always also reflect the systems imperatives of self-maintenance; in the delicate balancing of its measures, the system's intervention can remain merely therapeutic – that is, intended as a form of rehabilitation to restore the actor's adaptation to her/his designated function – or it can enhance her/his capacity for action and for an autonomous definition of the standards of well-being.

Whether we then become mere victims to these processes or can find in them a room for a possibility to raise to the status of competent interlocutors depends also on the intimacy of the relationship between us and our bodies: on our ability to listen to and read its signals, and to recognize its limits and its potential. Against the aseptic body of the medicine, we can only bring into being a living body, and so only if we have first learned its language. A body which is not inhabited by awareness and closeness can easily become an object for external manipulation; a body whose language is familiar and part of an ongoing dialogue is less prompt to be reduced to a sum of organs and apparatuses. It can feed our sense of personal rights, it can oppose a definition of health and well-being measured on external indicators, it can help us to become subjects of the cure, whenever we need to cope with illness.

6

On taking care

Healing the everyday

Intensive and unremitting care, unequalled in human history, is thus taken of our everyday lives; no longer fields of experience and of relations, our lives have turned into spaces for attention and manipulation by teams of specialists circumscribing problems and manufacturing solutions.

It is chiefly the policies pursued by the social and health services that are responsible for bringing this tendency to its current head. Preventive measures now operate according to a logic whereby a preliminary classification is drawn up of groups within the population, based on social, geographical, and epidemiological indicators decided in advance. Belonging to one of these groups and, hence, being directed through one of the preestablished channels for treatment of a problem (defined as either a pathology or the risk thereof) becomes the characteristic attached to every one of us, marking our individual life-histories thereafter.

Social relations are recategorized as 'problems' or 'pathologies', and the therapeutic measures taken to deal with them have extended their scope of application to cover most diverse fields. Sexual relations, the family, child-rearing, the school – in all these sectors messages of alarm are detected and measures taken in response abound.

The realm of sexual and interpersonal relationships is emblematic of this process. The relationship as a problem, the difficulties we encounter in meeting the standards of behaviour imposed on us, and our constant need to compare actual experience to the images prescribed and disseminated by various social agencies, add to our uncertainty and conspire to assign us to some category of pathology or other.

Thus we 'discover' that we are afflicted by previously altogether unsuspected problems. And even before we in due course enter the appropriate circuit of treatment, we have already enlisted the ready services of a prepackaged diagnostic apparatus, setting in motion a subtle process of self-labelling. Unavoidably, then, the intervention of specialists, experts, and advisers becomes necessary in order to permit better diagnostic definition of the problems thus brought to light, and eventually their possible 'solution'.

In education, the family, and socialization, the pedagogic relationship often becomes transformed into a therapeutic one. Whatever the learning or communicative deficiency, it is interpreted as a psychological or social-relational difficulty, and a process of sectorial treatment is launched which commonly forms only the first stage in the long history of intervention.

We apply these same criteria in our use of self-administered medication. We are constantly bombarded by health-care messages which alter our perceptions of our states of health and illness, deepening our unease concerning ourselves and our bodies: 'Am I ill, considering I've got the symptoms described in the medical column of the newspaper?' 'Should I look after my skin like the expert on the television tells me to?' 'Why didn't I think about improving my diet before?' The self-administration of medication gives us control over an ever-increasing field of uncertainty where all we can rely on is the advice of experts. We may remain unaware, of course, that it is very often these same experts who were responsible for the causes of our bewilderment in the first place.

All this has led to the wholesale therapeutization of everyday life, so that it now seems more imperative to heal life than to live it. The extension of prevention by means of the codified definition of pathologies and of risk groups intensifies the labelling process. Because of the predominantly diagnostic function of preventive measures, the circuit through which the 'case' must pass within the system becomes increasingly complex: treatment of the problem is handed from specialist to specialist and generally resolves itself in the interminable extension of the always more sophisticated diagnostic function, without any effective therapeutic action being taken.

The labelling applied by preventive policies and by screening inevitably upsets the mental and emotional equilibrium of the persons involved. Moreover, the users of these services often suffer from harmful psychological effects which increase their need for help (after hospitalization or a traumatic gynaecological examination, for example). Lastly, also the personnel working in these services are subjected to a high degree of stress, so that health care workers 'burned out' by the emotional overload of their profession require help as well.

The market for health goods and for information extends the range of our perception of pathology and induces us to measure our behaviour and relationships against standards of normality and well-being. The agencies

healing practices always fail to satisfy actual demand. As regards the social and psychological needs underlying therapeutic practice, this implies that our healing needs are never entirely unambiguous, never wholly reducible to their overt form; otherwise we would be forced to maintain that whatever a society institutionalizes as its official medicine unerringly provides an adequate response to the problem of illness. The circumstance that non-institutionalized therapeutic practices continue to exist, that they often satisfy a significant proportion of the existing demand, is proof of the fact that such a demand is really not what it appears to be. There is a component in our need for healing which contains other, latent meanings; and it is these meanings that official medicine leaves unattended but which parallel practices often address beyond the question of clinical effectiveness, rather equipping us with a capacity for symbolic elaboration.

Although the mere existence of parallel healing methods in the society is then nothing new, in the last twenty-five years alternative medicine has been popularized to a dramatic effect in the wake of other innovative cultural phenomena, new movements, and general changes in customs and behaviour. The similarity between alternative therapeutic practices and social movements is the tendency of both of them to utilize residual materials from society's cultural heritage. When a process of innovation begins but we lack the words to identify the new, we often find it necessary to ransack our cultural attic for the language, practices, and symbols required to give voice to needs for which suitable names do not exist as yet.

We act in this way in our personal lives as well, when we find ourselves in a novel, unexpected situation and lack the ready-made words prepared to express its meaning. We customarily deal with novelty by applying known and familiar words to unfamiliar things until the new reality has assumed its own distinctive shape, compelling us to coin the terms with which to describe it.

The same process is apparent in the revival of interest in traditional medicine. Of all the cultural material available to us, we selectively appropriate those elements which have the capacity of lending intuitive and approximate form to new needs. It is against precisely this creative activity in the changing context of a complex society that we must look at the current resurrection and mass diffusion of practices which, some for centuries, others for millennia, have otherwise been confined to their inconspicuous and feeble life in the historical and cultural margins of our society; had they rather proven themselves to be actually effective and offering a significant therapeutic alternative, their discovery and general revaluation could have begun many years earlier.

Forms of noninstitutional medicine continued to exist in small separate enclaves for centuries. Recently, however, they have attracted renewed interest that has consolidated in the enormous appeal they today exert, and, having first been properly recycled and given new currency, they have since exploded onto the market as a true mass phenomenon. By the same token a renewed interest has been addressed to forms of medicine which stayed alive in the 'non developed' societies and were long labelled as 'magic' by the Western scientific medicine. This revival of traditional practices has taken place as a response to a distinct cultural need – a fact whose recognition shall determine whether or not we can move on from the futile exercise of mere comparison between the contents of different therapeutic techniques to a more revealing analysis of such seemingly anachronistic practices. Through an examination of the ways our needs have changed, we can better gain an idea of why traditional medicine arouses our interest in post-traditional society, and why they are often so much as perceived to provide alternatives to official medicine. Such an analysis can contribute to an understanding of these practices, regardless of the evaluation of their effectiveness from a medical-scientific point of view. This can be obviously useful in clinical terms, but it does not explain the new popularity of traditional practices.

To begin with, the unprecedented availability of resources for investing in our self-realization has made us more attentive and sensitive to the conditions of our existence, inducing us to assume more direct responsibility for our own health. Secondly, illnesses seem more controllable and less fatal, but also more closely tied to social life and to its disequilibria: the illnesses of our times are characteristically associated with a significant weakening of the organism's defence mechanism. Faced with these new forms of 'epidemic', which have moved in to replace the scourges of the past, the limitations of official medicine become increasingly evident.

Modern medicine developed on the basis of a linear, causal paradigm which linked the symptom with a cause whose removal constituted the cure. As a result of the specialization and compartmentalization of medical theory and practice, the body is now treated as a bundle of functionally interconnected organs and apparatuses. Dysfunction is seen as a pathological phenomenon to be treated as a symptom, or else traced in a linear fashion to other organs and the apparatuses connected with them. The symptom, again, is taken as an obstacle to be removed so that the organ can function properly again.

In reaction to the evident shortcomings of this approach, one section of the scientific community has proposed a systemic paradigm which profoundly alters our perception of the process which underlies sickness and healing. The symptom, according to the new view, is not something to be eradicated; it signals a correlated set of causes, it is the starting point of a circular process gone awry that requires correction. This approach seems to revive, in the disenchanted formulae of scientific thought, the traditional view which regarded illness as a breakdown in harmony and an interruption in the cosmic process. Surprisingly to many, traditional wisdom today merges with a systemic vision to remind us that the malfunction is not confined to the organ but affects the individual as a whole, and that it is often only by means of the symptom that a person can express her/his discomfort or suffering.

Noninstitutional medicine is part of this cultural picture and contributes to its evolution. It, at least temporarily, seems equipped to respond adequately to new needs. The humanistic and spiritualistic values expressed by alternative medicine encourage the patient to assume responsibility for her/his illness, satisfying thereby people's demand for well-being and awareness. Moreover, many forms of traditional medicine operate within an energy-based conceptual framework which stresses the continuity between man, community, and cosmos, and focuses attention on the environmental and social dimensions of sickness and healing. Thus, paradoxically, traditional medicine contains aspects that are seemingly more modern than the hyperspecialized fragmentation of the official medicine they seek to supplant. Finally, the characteristic holistic and circular pattern – the idea, that is, of global interdependence – to which all traditional healing methods conform corresponds to the new systems paradigm emerging in contemporary sciences.

Standing in opposition as an alternative to official medicine and benefiting from its failures and inadequacies, noninstitutional healing methods have shown demonstrable cultural capability of satisfying contemporary needs. Their function, however, no doubt remains a temporary one: they will persist until traditional contents and practices have been incorporated into an overall redefinition of our concept of health and illness that alters the role and the instruments of medicine. The catalytic function performed by noninstitutional practices is also helping to draw up a different paradigm of medicine which recognizes the diversity of levels and the plurality of its own instruments.

Diagnostic procedures, for example, have made a major contribution to the evolution of modern medicine. With the highly sophisticated instruments now available, detailed and, in certain cases, extremely accurate diagnoses can be made. The problem, however, is that very often the process stops at diagnosis, leaving the sick tragically unable to cope with their illnesses or else condemned to an interminable sequence of symptomatic treatment when they are not faced with the dramatic choice of often unnecessary surgery. Thus the way has been paved for a different integration of diagnosis and therapy which respects people and their responsibility for their own health.

Another strength of modern medicine is its ability to handle emergency situations involving extreme pathological states of an epidemic or traumatic nature. The programmed use of antibiotics along with advances in surgical technique and intensive care present us with further examples of the extreme efficacy of modern medicine. This exceptional capacity to deal with emergencies should nevertheless be combined with a day-to-day practice that ensures recovery, or at least relief, from the many common disorders that afflict us. The ancient medical principle of *primum non nocere* ('In the first place, do no harm') becomes once again highly relevant in a world where iatrogenic illnesses – those, that is, induced by medical treatment or drug abuse – are alarmingly on the increase.

A medicine consisting of both diagnostic precision and patient responsibility, of effective action in emergencies and successful treatment in everyday life, can only be based on a new conception of sickness and of health. The plurality of the languages and instruments of therapeutic practice must therefore be recognized, and the principle that different keys open different doors acknowledged. Noninstitutional medicine, for its own part, has contributed to the transformation now in progress, thanks to the substantial contents of what it has been able to offer, but still more importantly as an effect of what it helps us to imagine.

Another outlook

Another modern route to mental health is provided by psychotherapy. The increased popularity of this therapeutic technique has ensued in response to our general need for self-realization, and, more particularly, reflecting the internalization of the fact that we may today conceive of life as a choice among various possibilities, as the process of the discovery and fulfilment of our potentialities. The reverse side of the unconstrained freedom (and necessity) of choice, however, is the greater psychological stress induced by the multiple pressures of the complexity of our daily experience. The very diffusion and penetration of the services which medicalize our social and individual problems often provokes mental suffering within the institutional circuits of care provision.

Today, a broad range of therapeutic techniques cater to this widespread demand for psychological treatment and counselling. The various techniques of psychoanalysis are now flanked by family counselling, body therapies, humanistic-existential therapies, and behavioural therapies. This proliferation of mutually competing techniques obviously raises questions about the validity of their claims. There exists, however, a high degree of homogeneity among the factors which favour the success, or contribute to the failure, of therapeutic action: its outcome always depends on the nature of the personal encounter.

How therapists really behave in their immediate relationships with those seeking their help frequently differs considerably from what the theory tells them to do. The psychotherapeutic situation is about listening and welcoming, about a space and a time in which suffering is not denied but acknowledged. Listening encourages and amplifies the expression of mental distress, although it is difficult for the therapist to listen in a manner unaffected by the theory and by the therapist's desire to help the patient. Psychotherapy is a process which involves two consenting people; without this freedom the therapeutic situation cannot exist. It can only take place if it is brought about by, on the one side, a person willing to submit to it and, simultaneously as the other pole in the relationship, a therapist with her/his own goals, expectations, and fears.

In psychotherapy a person can be 'healed' in many different – indeed mysterious – ways. Patients, just as their therapists, do not know why they feel better or why their distress has been eased. The constant feature in all cases, however, is the change brought about by the therapy; a change which enables patients to recognize themselves as situated individuals endowed with existential capacities and limitations, and to assume responsibility for their place in reality, in all its physical, affective, mental, and spiritual dimensions. This, in fact, is the definition given to sickness and healing by traditional cultures. The individual is located within an order of things (physical-biological, social, and cosmic-spiritual) in which 'illness' always signals a breakdown in the articulation of its components. 'Healing' is possible only if equilibrium is reestablished and the circuit linking the individual with the cosmos reenacted.

For this to happen, however, the field has to be restructured: there must be a modification of the perception and definition of the patient's immediate situation responsible for her/his present suffering. Accordingly, it is this restructuring that the therapist helps to bring about.

The background to the therapeutic process is formed by the consensual nature of the relationship. Here lies a clear-cut difference between the therapeutic situation thus outlined and that obtaining in actual psychiatric treatment. There are, of course, social and organizational differences between psychotherapeutic practice and institutional psychiatric methods; equally evident are the difficulties involved in the application of psychotherapy in institutional settings when the nature of the suffering and its treatment is decided by others (family, institution, social context). Although institutional constraints are certainly an impediment to the growth of a consensual relationship of change, innovative psychiatric experiences have shown that the institutionalization of the therapeutic situation can nevertheless offer a number of advantages. Everything within the institutional setting may become therapeutic if the everyday context is suitably structured and if opportunities are created for patients to be listened to and welcomed, and for them to exercise their autonomy.

This argument extends beyond the institutional context. The 'healing' process usually continues well past the moment of institutional therapy; the relationship triggers something that happens elsewhere and which passes beyond 'therapy'. There are therapeutic events which coincide with life but which are only brought to light by the therapeutic relationship. Here too we find elements of traditional cultures: the idea that healing is always and only a collective undertaking, a rite which involves the community as a whole. The 'sick person' can be brought back to health since the rite reforges the bond between the individual, the group, and the universe – that is, between the individual and life.

Why and how psychotherapy works is difficult to say. Research into what takes place in its course is rarely conclusive in the sense of yielding absolute criteria of effectiveness. It does, however, show extremely clearly that the key element in the therapeutic process is the relationship: it is depending on the quality of the (sustained) encounter between the therapist and the patient that the success of psychotherapy is decided. The significant features of a successful therapist include authenticity, indicating the therapist's closeness to her/himself and awareness of her/his personal needs and goals; acceptance of the other, that is, the absence of the therapist's omnipotent ambition to substitute her/himself for the patient; and an ability to listen, that is, to provide the time and space for the 'sick person' to voice her/his distress. For patients, the key therapeutic variables are the ability to confront their weaknesses and to accept change as possible and desirable: this 'strength in weakness', this ability to entrust oneself to another while simultaneously relying on one's own resources, seems to be the decisive factor in any successful therapy.

Therapy produces a change of outlook in the sufferer, an altered perception of her/his self and the world. This shift of horizon, with the cognitive and affective consequences that it brings, does not take place in a vacuum but within a very special kind of relationship. We call it 'therapeutic' because it provides a privileged space and time in which the two poles of the relation can preserve their difference while proceeding in their ongoing communicative interaction. When otherness and communication, openness and closure, nearness and distance are not imposed but chosen, another way of looking at the world becomes possible.

By adopting this perspective, we are forced to abandon the causally based model of therapy. Mental distress and the possibility of alleviating it are always determined by a circular multiplicity of causes, all of which are present in the immediate context of the sufferer. Therapy addresses the person as a global whole. Dealing with mental illness cannot rely on a causal logic which stresses diagnostic aspects and considers present suffering to be the last link in a linear chain of events. Calling the linear causality model into question, however, is not to imply that we ought to forgo thinking that employs causes and connections, only that these linkages today have multiplied their quantity and intensity so that it no longer is possible to establish univocal relations among them.

Hence, the therapeutic relationship cannot be deduced from the models of scientific explanation; its unique features can never be wholly explained by the theory. It can be talked about – the therapist or the patient can recount the experience – and it can be the subject of scientific discourse which reassures therapists and ratifies them as members of their professional community; but it is nothing of this that brings the change about.

Recognizing the distance that separates therapeutic practice from the models that we use to describe and interpret it, marks the beginning of a new approach to the sufferer. That which we construct as a linguistic instrument or as an interpretative code constitutes a map, a language. Nevertheless, although it may account for events it can never translate them entirely. The therapeutic situation consists of a *circular relationship*: it depends on what flows back and forth between therapist and patient in a unique game of mutual expectations and fears, it involves the capacity or incapacity to establish contact, to listen and to make oneself heard.

Technique and fate

The inevitability of natural events seems increasingly subject to the conscious control by efficient technology, leaving fate today to assume the guise of whatever escapes the power of technique; we are thus compelled to recognize the shadow that delimits and interrogates our ability to cure. Fate reappears in the form of new pathologies which touch the deepest levels of our affects and relations, generating unforeseen effects on social processes. Society produces new forms of suffering which leave us without defence when technology misfires or fails to live up to its own promises.

In all the advanced industrialized countries of the world, the average birth rate at present is 1.5 children per woman, with minor variations from country to country (in demographic terms, two children per woman is equivalent to zero population growth). This means that the decline in the populations of the countries of the 'centre' is destined to accelerate, while the demographic explosion in the planet's 'peripheries' will continue, exerting enormous pressure on the more privileged areas (it is predicted that in the year 2000, the so-called Third World will represent 80 per cent of the world population; and that, of the whole population of the United States aged under 50, the inhabitants of African, Asiatic, and Hispanic origin will outnumber those of European ancestry). This enormous transformation in the social composition of the species will provoke dramatic alignments and conflicts, and will inevitably alter interstate relations at a planetary level as well as interethnic relations within individual countries. On a scale closer to individual experience, the fertility figures for the more advanced countries are flanked by clinical data that indicate a striking increase in the numbers of childless couples. The World Health Organization estimates the sterility rate in the most industrialized countries at 30 per cent, and the phenomenon seems bound to increase. Research also shows that, in the majority of cases, sterility is due to functional factors bound up with stress, pollution, and diet. In a sense, sterility thus represents the silence of the body, made mute by the clamour of civilization. The psychogenic and environmental origins of sterility are evident and force themselves to public consciousness: affluent society is beginning to undermine the bases of its own reproduction precisely at the moment when it felt reason to celebrate the triumph of research and the conquests of technology in the reproductive sphere.

Another phenomenon which has apparently escaped society's control is the renewed vigour of sexually transmitted diseases, of which acquired immunodeficiency syndrome (AIDS) is only the most dramatic and immediately dangerous instance. Before the menace of AIDS burst with such violence onto the public scene to capture the attention of the media and governments, epidemiological research had already reported a disquieting increase in other sexually transmitted diseases and the spread of once marginal infections which seem today to have developed a remarkable vigour.

Some moralists interpret the threat of an AIDS epidemic of alarming proportions either as divine retribution of a kind or as nature's punishment for the Promethean arrogance of our technological civilization. These dramatic pronouncements fit well with a society enamoured of the sensational and they provide excellent fodder for the media, but they are of little help for one who seriously seeks to understand the causes of these phenomena and, above all, decide how to deal with them.

As regards AIDS, attention has focused chiefly on the perception of the disease by the collective imagination and on its effects on everyday life, in particular as regards sexual mores. But beneath these more visible levels of the phenomenon there lie hidden processes which vitally affect the functioning of contemporary systems.

There are, first of all, the systemic disturbances created by an event potentially able to trigger a series of chain reactions in various subsystems (health care system, information, the family, the school, the political system, and so forth).

Next, there are those processes which marginalize entire social categories: homosexuals, for instance, who find themselves deprived of their recently acquired social autonomy by a stigma against which they have no appeal; or drug addicts, especially those living in the alienation of the great cities, where their already dramatic situation is aggravated even further.

Again, there are those processes of cultural coding and normative definition which covertly but effectively issue through their repercussions in health policies and emergency measures. A prime example of these is the way in which categories at risk are established. What is in question is a cultural coding process which transfers into policy the already tenuous certainties of epidemiological research. The selection of categories at risk may bear major consequences on the legal system and on forms of social control. It is, nevertheless, a selection based on a fundamental ambiguity which has gone largely unnoticed. Although our knowledge of AIDS is still inadequate, we nevertheless know that the danger of infection is essentially linked to certain types of behaviour, and therefore with a set of predominantly individual variables. Prevention and control take very different forms according to whether the target is individual behaviour or whether such behaviour is attributed to entire social categories, typically in a process of administrative codification which flouts logic and ignores the truth while undoubtedly streamlining procedures as a result.

There is, finally, the subjective experience of the disease, living with its visible signs and with the disquieting presence of risk: those who have actually fallen ill, their relatives, the HIV positive, social and health workers – all exposed in various ways to suffering and to a dramatic confrontation with death and the limits of medical knowledge and skill. Modern hospital systems have done their best to eliminate death as a cultural experience, and to this extent they also lack the means to handle suffering, which retains its physical referent and presence but above all is always an affective and relational condition. The same is true for terminal cancer patients.

Being present and listening, the ability to give companionship to the sufferer and to respect in silence her/his inevitable encounter with death – these have become rare qualities in the desacralizing culture of the metropolises;

they are qualities that conflict with the rhythms, sounds, and signs of the urban universe.

Yet, today as much as in the past, these qualities are needed by those approaching the ineluctable end and experiencing, directly or indirectly, the grip and the vertigo of impotence in the face of death.

Word and ritual

In the traditional world, illness was an alien presence, the invasion of the cosmic order by a dark force. It was akin to death, and yet it could be approached and even tamed like a wild animal through the mediation of ritual which restored the illness to the sacred order and utilized its powers to produce a new equilibrium in the individual, in the community, and in the universe.

We live in the age witnessing the paradox of an apparent victory over disease: just as we have begun to believe in our ability to control the dark forces of nature that produce disease, new scourges arrive to afflict us that can be identified with effects and properties of precisely the same powers with which we thought we had already won the battle. The inevitability of the illnesses generated by civilization produces twofold alienation: the alienation within each one of us in our relationship with suffering, and the alienation attributable to the condition in which the treatment of illness is entirely entrusted to external and impersonal apparatuses.

Illness thus becomes once again a profoundly estranged and uncontrollable experience. In our epoch, however, there is no ritualistic means left to intervene in and to reestablish the bond with the sacred order that it could still ensure in traditional societies. We no longer possess the language with which to name pain, and we place our hopes in the mechanics of technology. Pain is no longer the trial that pits us against fate, as with the heroes of antiquity. Nor is suffering the price of redemption it was in the Christian tradition. All we have left is our faith in technology, which only yields us disappointments as much as it first raises our hopes. Modern medicine's sensational discoveries, its extraordinary advances, have little relevance to our everyday pain. And where technology is lacking or fails to deliver for us personally, who can succour us? Of what value are the triumphs of medical research if they do not effectively address our own illness when it appears, if they lie beyond the concrete circumstances of our suffering? For when we are touched by pain and illness, they take shape as intimately ours alone and no one else's.

What kind of a contact, then, can we reestablish with illness in societies which defy death with the full power of their technological apparatus? The lost link can only be forged again as a new cultural process, as the capacity to measure ourselves against the limit and against death. While – and precisely for that reason – the various gods no longer are with us to provide protection against affliction, pain and its relief can become human experiences which we can learn to see as meaningful. We need to invent the words and the ritual, recognize that we are alone in our suffering, and rebuild the links between us and others, between us and the world. Illness, be it serious or minor, which reveals to us our mortality may lead us back to the roots of our personal uniqueness and may open us up to the universe through the recognition that we are only small fragments of everything that exists.

Therapy, too, is part of this process and is equally put to the test. As the act of taking care, it establishes a paradoxical relationship between sufferer and helper. It is only possible to provide care if the responsibility of the 'patient' can be counted upon, and only if the one to provide the care can assume responsibility for the cure. The patient, for her/his part, can only be taken care of if s/he trusts the carer, but the decision to do so remains with her/him alone.

The second aspect of the paradox concerns the space of therapy, which is simultaneously everyday space and a space apart; the arena of real life and the realm of magic, where unique and unrepeatable contact is established between the individual and her/his limit, and where overcoming or transforming this limit is made possible by some form of ritual. Therapy takes place within the spaces of everyday routine (hospitals, care services), but healing occurs only if another space, the inner space of trust and hope and the space of a human meaningful relationship between the sufferer and the care-giver, is inhabited.

Finally, the time of therapy is likewise marked by a paradox: it is biographical and social time and yet it is timeless time, with events following one another not according to customary chronology but according to the unpredictable sequencing of the sufferer's biological and psychological experience. The cadence and delays of the therapeutic process are those imposed by organizational constraints, personal and social time obligations; but healing occurs when another time takes effect, when the 'right moment' has come for the sufferer and for the healer.

How can the two sides of the paradox be reconciled in a disenchanted world, where the sacred no longer connects the poles of the arduous experience that confronts us with the limit and the possibility of death? How can we both count on the responsibility of the sufferer and simultaneously assume it? How can real space be aligned with magical space? How can we pass from clock or calendar time to the time of inner experience? To such questions there are no unequivocal answers, and they stay with us to frame the definition of health and sickness in our culture. They compel us to seek out and experiment with the words, practices and rituals with which to create the conditions for cure.

Despite the enormous potency of the means deployed to eradicate it, illness has not disappeared from the scenario of the possible. Faced with illness, we can either behave like sacrificial victims, unwittingly subjected to a causal event which we leave for others to define, or we can approach it in a manner similar to the way traditional cultures confronted the experience of the sacred – the difference lying in our disenchanted awareness. Facing our limits and the confrontation with the possible death demands a measure of awe and respect, for which we have lost the language. But even in the poverty of language, as we encounter our limit, we cannot today avert the risk implicit in a choice where it is our capacity to produce meaning out of our actions, suffering, or death that is at stake. We cannot help but exist as individuals, nor can we escape the responsibility of taking care of ourselves.

Therapy, whatever form it takes, faces the same option. It can function as an instrument of external regulation, blinded by its illusion of omnipotence. Alternatively, it can accompany the sufferer in her/his perilous confrontation with the limit and the possibility of overcoming it.

For those who suffer and for those who take care of them, illness can be a dogged struggle against an invisible enemy. But it can also become a passage through the magic circle which opens the way to finitude and freedom.

7

The abyss of difference

The encounter with the other

Much talk is devoted today to address the great concerns of our time, individualism and the fragmentation of social life, above all in the great metropolises of the world. The cities create 'lonely crowds', isolated individuals deprived of their ability to communicate and, as a result, suffering under conditions of anomie in which mass conformism and manipulation structure all social life. Metropolitan culture, it is reported, is narcissistic; it produces people who relate only to themselves, people in search of personal well-being but unable to establish meaningful relationships with others. While we can agree with much in this description, in our everyday lives we nevertheless encounter others in important ways that are not immediately visible; consequently, the texture of our relationships is far richer than what the accounts of social atomization would have us believe.

Individualism is an attribution that usually defines in a negative sense processes and behaviours which disguise other meanings. In our daily lives, in fact, we know that the variety and abundance of the stimuli we encounter at any given moment often have the effect of expanding the individual dimension of our action, in the sense of increasing our awareness of what we do. In present-day society, we have unparalleled resources at our disposal with which to affirm ourselves and recognize ourselves as individuals. First, education and the circulation of information offer us hitherto unknown opportunities for knowledge-acquisition and action. Secondly, through generalized inclusion in a common language we have become an integral part of universalistic codes of communication. Thirdly, civil and political participation expected of us as citizens requires of us the exercise of decision-making capacities which rely on our individual autonomy of choice.

These resources obviously remain unequally distributed, but yet, at the

societal level, we may with reason recognize ourselves as individuals, defining ourselves as distinct subjects of action independent of the bonds of our
memberships, our social or geographical location, or the constraints of the
past. Industrial society had already witnessed locality, language, and religion lose their primary function of identification, only so as to make way for
categories, such as those based on occupational position or political
membership, into which individuals entered by their own choice. Today,
however, nor do these criteria any longer prove sufficient enough to allow
for an answer to the question that we increasingly address to ourselves:
'Who am I?' It is within our individual dimension that we must from now
on seek the answer.

The question of personal identity was only of limited significance in
traditional systems, and it was in any case settled within the existing
social order and its rituals. For the Guayaki people of Amazonia, for
example, who stand at the other cultural extreme from our mighty
technological society, it is practically meaningless. For these small bands
of nomadic hunters traversing the harsh environment from which they
draw their daily sustenance, the survival of the group is the paramount
concern overriding all others. This imperative produces a rigid division
of labour based on gender, along with close mutual dependence between
the individuals of the group. There is little room for individual difference
outside such order, and the social constraint must be maintained at any
cost. In the event of breakdown of its internal solidarity, the group will
not be able to survive. It is only in the ritual song of the hunters gathered around the evening campfire that the question 'Who am I?' may be
broached. By celebrating his personal feats as a hunter through song,
each individual speaks of himself as a distinct individual, but only within
the circumscribed symbolic space allotted for the purpose, and thus
without putting in question the premises upon which the existence of the
group depends. And in any case, the opportunity is available for the men
only.

This example of a culture so far removed from ours holds up a mirror to
our own experience. The question of personal identity occupies a large part
of our lives, and we devote considerable amounts of time and energy to
answering it, using the various means at our disposal (education, self-reflection, care for ourselves, psychotherapy, development of our personal
potential, creative activities). In this, the pattern of our interpersonal relations is engaged in a process whereby its logic is profoundly altered. The
distant society of the Guayaki hunters offers us a reversed image of this
pattern: A taboo prohibits a hunter from eating the animal he has killed,
with each hunter allowed to feed only on meat that others have procured.

The relationships between men and women are similarly based on an inter-weaving system of exchange which reinforces the bond within the group. Survival of the group thus depends on the maintenance of the exchange and on the strength of the social constraint: each individual exists because s/he can depend on all the others. The fact that today we can define ourselves as distinct persons fully aware of our individuality, brings along with it a profound transformation of our relationships: they become not just a necessity or constraint but also a field of choice.

Yet it is precisely the relationship with the other that enables us to recognize the possibility of, and choose, difference. A relationship exists when whatever it is that distinguishes us from the others is accepted and used as the basis for communication – a process which always draws upon something shared in order to discover and to affirm diversity. The possibility of choice introduces contingency and risk into our relationships (whether affective, familial, or neighborly) with others, and turns them into a field of investment and self-reflection. Fragmentation and isolation are the dark side of this process, the result of our incapacity to choose or to withstand the strain of communication.

Encountering the other is to expose oneself to the abyss of difference. Every day, otherness and communication put us to the test. As we search for relationships, we encounter the enormous range of difference that the others constitute for us in the society, particularly when the variety of cultures, groups and individuals becomes even more evident; difference which attracts us precisely because of the richness it contains, but which is also fraught with risk and instant danger. The difference of the others, that is, challenges us in two ways. Firstly, it confronts us with ourselves, with our limit but also with our uniqueness. Secondly, it forces us to a constant search for a bridge, to seek a common point of contact, to construct the language and rules of the exchange.

This enterprise, however, may fail, and experiencing otherness may well prove impossible from the outset. On the one hand, we may end up experiencing a loss of our identity and, as it were, blend with the other. The attempted encounter dissipates in a loss of boundaries under the impact of the invasion of our territory by the thousand differences that surround us. We really become one, no one, a thousand, as each and everyone attracts us, belongs to us, seduces us. Or, on the other hand, we may remain locked in our difference, unable to take the risk of exposing ourselves to the unknown that the other represents for us. For encountering another always entails putting into question something of ourselves and of our uniqueness and venturing into an unknown land only to discover what we lack: exposing oneself to otherness implies a challenge to one's self-sufficiency and the recognition that the other is different precisely because s/he possesses what we do not have and what we may need, and vice versa.

But, although we might wish to entrust ourselves fully to the encounter, to become entirely understood, we will inevitably realize that a part of ourselves is never captured by the exchange, that the other's understanding never wholly encompasses us; even the best will in the world is never enough for us to be able to feel completely at home in the territory of the other. The repeated experience of such shortfalls in communication adds to the existential burdening of the encounter with the other, commonly resulting in a withdrawal into cynical aloofness, into renunciation of the frustrated aims, or, in the most serious case, into the closedness of the self.

The hardship and the joy of the encounter thus stand in a delicate equilibrium. The challenge of otherness is met depending on whether or not we can adopt the point of view of the other without losing ourselves in so doing. Empathy, a term which has now entered everyday language, indicates closeness to the other and the ability to see things from the other's point of view. But this is to go only halfway; protect us from emptiness and loss. Without an ability to remain anchored in a self that is our own and to bridge the void between that self and the other's, there is no encounter but only benevolence, or mere goodwill. The encounter brings two regions of meaning together, two fields of energy at different frequencies which we adjust until they resonate with each other. The encounter is *sym-pathy*; it is *com-passion*, feeling-with-another; it is the discovery that meaning does not belong to us but is rather given in the encounter itself, although, at the same time, only we can create it.

Hence, encountering the other is to embark on a journey into the vertigo of meaning. Everyday life is the space of presentness and loss where the others guide us in our journey, even if, to be sure, they are also mirages in our scope of vision interfering to lead us astray.

Of all instances of difference, two are inevitable and affect us more than others: age and gender. They represent fundamental difference, permanent otherness which serves as a metaphor for any other difference. Being young and being old, being male and being female, are the poles of an irreducible difference which can teach us how to meet the challenge of the encounter.

Being young, being old

Analyzing the relationship between the generations, between the beginning and the end of the life-cycle, is to focus on a difference that leaves no margins of uncertainty and which brings the polarity of presentness/absence to the fore. Irreducible and never entirely communicable as a lived dimension, the experience of presentness and absence is also a social phenomenon embodied in the history of the generations and their mutual relationships. This history can be observed and described, mindful of the fact that in so doing we are also addressing the core question about the relation to otherness in our culture.

Memory and project, past and future, feed our fragile present. In the experience of aging, with the past expanding until it is dissolved and the future dwindling to its vanishing point, the link between the two grows more fragile than at any other moment of our life. Today, the prolongation of the average life-span, with the consequent aging of the population, has transformed old age from a cultural reservoir of wisdom for younger generations into a social problem of dramatic proportions. Growing old and being old raise a shadow of disquiet over our society, radiant with happiness and health in celebration of the splendors of youth and physical efficiency. Our culture deliberately shuns exposure to the prospect of loss, illness, and physical decay by confining them to separate enclaves, or by investing them with a spurious commercial glamour. Joyful and energetic old people smile from our TV sets advertising new goods, while a large share of the population over 65 in even the most affluent countries ends its life in hospitals and public assistance institutions. The extent to which this denial has been completed raises serious questions concerning our ability to look after our old people – and therewith after ourselves as the old people of the future.

This, however, is not to imply that we are untroubled by old age, nor that we have failed to arrange for the care of our elderly. Yet our general attitude towards this section of the population shows the reductive tendency to treat it as either a social nuisance or an occasion for the expression of finer sentiments. It is as if there were no ethical necessity compelling us to preoccupy ourselves with the old people; only the disconcerted notion that they constitute a problem, or the compassion they arouse in us. We react to them the same way we respond to the predicament of the Amazonian rain forest: as an object of impropriety somehow distantly committed to us all, with moreover a vague element of threat to it, yet nothing that directly affects our daily lives; or we are genuinely moved by the cruel fate of the helpless losers cleared out of the way of civilization and progress. In our treatment of the old people, a logic of either alarm or welfare predominates. Aging and old age, however, acquire a different ethical weight when considered as a cultural process confronting us with otherness. As such, they unfold as a phenomenon which has a symbolic function as a message, for it tells us something about our society as a whole. Manifest concern for the elderly is not merely a measure of social welfare required to deal with an unavoidable nuisance; it is a way of recognizing and safe-guarding meaning, an ethical option which induces us to face the problem of choice and the risk of otherness.

The problem of old age occupies an increasingly large share of our atten-tion because of its practical gravity and empirical scope. Still, it remains uncomprehended as a *signal* and as an *appeal* – as a reminder pointing out to us the frailty of our existence and, at the same time, a guide through the labyrinth of absence. The reduction of life-chances, physical decay, disease, and the possible decline of the higher faculties underscore old people's lack of presentness. Among the many images of old age, perhaps the most evocative is the saturnine theme of loss: the gradual weakening or collapse of the vital functions, the dimming of memory. Alzheimer's disease, for example, is a stigma which today marks the condition of an ever-growing number of the old and not so old. The loss of short-term memory inter-rupts the temporal sequence of actions and erases spatial referents. Disoriented and unable to recognize her/his own gestures due to the fading memory, the sufferer gradually drifts into terminal bewilderment. Alzheimer's disease is not the classic senile dementia that used to affect only the older age groups; today premature aging strikes people at a much earlier age.

The theme of loss indeed stands as a symbol of the problems of our age. Goaded by the fading of hope into the territory of inertia and of absence, old people in modern society seem destined to lose their ability to focus on what is most tangible and most immediate in experience: the perception of one's being-here as rooted in time, as the conjunction of memory and project; as the relationship between self and others and among the differ-ent components of personal experience. Presentness is the perception of the instant and of duration, an encounter with history and with possibility: it disappears when the past fades, the future shrinks, and the present becomes a vacuous repetition.

The unravelling of the capacity for presentness alienates individuals from both themselves and the world: cognitive incompetence, obsolescence or the social uselessness of accumulated wisdom, and the cancellation of the past only represent the time-sedimented effects of the withdrawal and closure into which old people are now forced by complexity.

Old people are increasingly excluded from the new know-how. But the experience of no longer knowing how to do things rapidly becomes the more general feeling of not knowing what to do at all, which is one of the most dramatic forms of bewilderment. Usually, when we face a new problem, at least part of what we already know points to the direction we must move in: then the fact of partially not knowing triggers change.

However, when the loss is rapid and complete as in the case of the elderly, people are left groping in total darkness.

A situation of accelerated and unremitting change spurns everything that old people have learned in a different and by now culturally distant age, while they themselves find it impossible to keep pace with new knowledge. Yet this is only the most visible aspect of the experience of cognitive incompetence. More profound and more dramatic is the realization that accumulated knowledge cannot be handed down because it is no longer of interest to anyone.

Thus, life-history can no longer provide an anchorage for a person's identity, although individual biography still provides one of the principal reference systems in its construction. To be meaningful and to fulfil this function, biography requires spatio-temporal coordinates which are both internal and external. The old people's loss of their external moorings in complex societies is mainly the result of changes in everyday technologies – which comprise not just industrial technologies in the narrow sense but that vast range of machinery which makes up the current instrumentation of our lives. If using a computer may be beyond an old person's capabilities, apparently much more banal problems, like opening a bank account or using a key card to open an automatic door, as well become tasks of daunting complexity. But also ecological change and the transformation of physical space and of the territorial fabric erase points of reference and blur the meaning of the spatio-temporal maps by which we plot our movements and locate our bodies. The conditions for the fundamental experience of bewilderment are thus prepared.

The internal moorings of identity also slip and fracture, primarily as a result of a widening cultural divide between the moment when the experience was acquired and the actual moment when it can be represented in the memory, between the time of the action and its remembering. The clouding of memory is not just a neurological process, and the spread of Alzheimer's disease in contemporary societies cannot be attributed to biological factors alone. The dimming of memory derives both from the disorientation I have just discussed and from the cultural distance between action and remembering. The other side to this loss of inner anchorage links up with language. In the wake of the loss of shared frameworks of experience and meaning, the words old people employ to name things are no longer necessarily understood in the sense with which they are used by those who utter them. The experience which ties a person to her/his life-history cannot be articulated, which produces a kind of cultural autism. Finally, affective isolation similarly participates in the deprivation of life-history of its anchoring function. Affective bonds enable us to recognize ourselves through them, and the more the isolation increases the more the identification processes miscarry, the more they turn into contentless formulae. Bewilderment, the clouding of memory, temporal and linguistic incoherence, the affective neutralization of the processes of identification – all these undermine the ability of old people today to draw on their personal life-histories in pursuing the question 'Who am I?'

What is preserved from experience, therefore, is but a mechanical repertoire of gestures and words which progressively lose their meaning. The overall outcome of these processes is withdrawal, closure, and repetition. Many of the geriatric pathologies described in predominantly biological or psychiatric terms derive, in fact, from this profound cultural change – a change which not only affects old people but is symptomatically present in their very predicament.

Old people signal the loss of being-here as the possibility, if not a fatal tendency, to which we are exposed by our culture. Old people in complex societies speak to us of meaning, of presentness and of its limits – of their absence and ours.

Presentness, possibility, and loss

Analysis of loss, as in a game of opposites, suggests a line of reasoning based on presentness and possibility. The social relationship and the dynamics that link the generations together were essential to the existence of past societies and contemporary complex systems are losing the capacity of keeping alive the connection between old and young people. Let us, then, shift our attention from what was discussed above to the other pole of this opposition: the one represented by fullness as opposed to emptiness, by the expansion of the possible, by the saturation of the present. While these are attributes that obviously represent traits usually associated with youth, a more careful analysis counsels caution.

In complex systems, being young seems much less a biological condition than a cultural definition. Uncertainty, mobility, temporariness, willingness to accept change have been conventionally attributed to youth, conceived as the transitional phase between childhood and adulthood. Today these characteristics seem to extend beyond the biological constraint of young age, and they assume the form of cultural connotations widely appropriated by people well advanced into adulthood. Thus youth as a condition seems to continue beyond any particular age limit and becomes a suspension of every stable engagement, a sort of nomadism through time, space, and cultures. Styles of dress, musical genres, and group memberships function as provisional and variable languages with which identity is established and signals of recognition are projected to the outside.

The surfeit of culturally available possibilities expands the confines of the imaginary and incorporates entire regions of experience once marked by biological, corporeal, and material determinants into the realm of the symbolic. Everything becomes appearance and image, so that experience is increasingly less a datum and increasingly more a cognitive and relational construct; increasingly less a 'fact' and increasingly more a 'work in progress' or a 'fiction'.

It is young people who most directly experience the allure of the expansion of the possible. A nearly unlimited extension of the cognitive and emotional field, the reversibility of choices and decisions, the replacement of the material contents of experience with symbolic constructs – it is apparently these that constitute the new frontiers of a youthful condition, defined more by cultural styles and languages than by age.

What, then, is experience? Youth culture apparently assigns preference to reading about reality through its images over looking at it, to telling itself about the world over touching it. Overlapped and invaded by the symbolic appeal of the possible, experience is in danger of being overwhelmed by a limitless present of extreme fragility and of becoming shrunken to the dimensions of the instant: bereft of roots because of the poverty of memory, and holding reservations about the future as a consequence of disenchantment. Experience dissolves into the imaginary, and the test of the harsh realities of life provokes frustration, boredom, and apathy. The new sufferings and the new pathologies of the young people are triggered by the dissolution of their temporal perspectives.

Also at this pole of the life-course presentness seems today fragile and threatened. Precisely here, where abundance, fullness, and acquisition seem to predominate, we find emptiness, repetition, and loss of reality. A time which offers the possible in excess becomes a timeless possibility; that is, a pure phantasm of duration. Time may become an empty envelope, an interminable delay spent waiting for Godot.

The limit thus becomes the necessary condition for the permanence of meaning. Where there is no encounter with a limit there can be no experience or communication; without awareness of loss and otherness as the constitutive dimensions of being-here there is no human action or relationship. It is here that the extreme poles of the life-cycle – youth and old age – can be recognized as being connected by an unbreakable bond. The relation between them becomes the necessary condition for the survival of the species within the scenario of complexity. The relationship between the generations is explicitly transformed from a biological datum into a cultural reality. Awareness of the limit and loss can constitute presentness as the ability to care and to project, as responsibility towards others and towards the past, and towards the future. If old people testify with their bodies and with their memories to this appeal, then to take care of them is to keep alive the possibility of meaning for us all.

Experience of the limit gives us a chance to review our existence; it creates opportunities for change and regeneration. This experience may be humanly 'mediated' in the encounter with old people through listening. The exposure to a face-to-face encounter with that part of ourselves which we conceal from sight and keep in isolation (the old people we shall ourselves eventually become) may result in a change of outlook: a different presentness.

Today, the relationship between youth and old age has to be seen as fundamentally different from what it used to be in the past. It is increasingly distinguished by freedom and by risk, by contingency and by choice, for there is no biological constraint left that makes it necessary. If the encounter with the limit is the cultural and ethical link that ties the two extreme poles of the life-cycle together, it is also the condition for change: only the experience of the limit can generate the metamorphoses that young and old people need. It is a way of preventing time from collapsing into a one-dimensional sequence of mere points, into a sum of timeless moments.

We need the experience of the limit visually and corporeally mediated by the presence of old people – as that section of the population most in contact with loss, pain, and death – contrary to the pressure exerted by our culture for them to camouflage and deny the reality of any such limitations. Our efforts to prolong our life-chances, in fact, disguise also a subtle tendency to promote an image of the youthful elderly who carry the weight of their years with athletic nonchalance. This illusion of eternity, however, distracts from the beneficial confrontation with the reality of the limit, our only source of hope.

The relationship between presentness and absence, between opportunity and loss, is a dilemma that our culture will inevitably fail to resolve. No policy for the old, even the most enlightened, can hope to escape it. All we can do is produce partial solutions. Between, on the one hand, the aspiration to omnipotence inducing the illusory dream of completely autonomous elderly without any problems, and, on the other, the need to cope with dependence, loss, and the existence of social dustbins, from which we can never entirely extricate ourselves, there lies the concrete space of our action: again, an encounter with the limit is the wisdom which, all our neglect notwithstanding, old people still transmit to us.

Male/female

Besides age, another extremely broad field of uncertainty, one which today covers a large area of our experience, concerns the relationships between the sexes and the male/female difference. Going back in time, even just a few generations, we detect a distinct change that has taken place in the social definition of the sexes, in the ways the men and women perceive each other, in the division of labour within the family and the couple. Yet, at the more intimate level of interpersonal relations, relationships between the sexes do not seem to have changed to any marked extent. Some generations ago, the human problems of love, of closeness and distance, and of the joys and difficulties of communication were not significantly different from the dilemmas of today. People fell in love, they were happy to be loved in return and suffered if they were not; men and women already confronted the problem of choosing a partner as a risk and a responsibility.

What has profoundly changed (at a different pace in individual countries) is the cultural framework surrounding the relationships between the sexes – love in particular. Only fifty years ago in many industrial countries, there still existed a cultural framework which provided a guarantee for these relationships and grounded individual certainties. Once a couple had formed it hardly ever split up; those rare occasions when it did, were dramatic experiences and numbered, along with bereavement or emigration, among the crucial events in a person's life-history. In everyday life, the relationships between the sexes, and the affective relationships in particular, were institutionally guaranteed and confirmed by the family order, and sustained by a stable network of kinship and friends. Even when the choice of partner was not dictated by familial constraints, it was still strongly influenced by the norms and the circumstances of the kinship group, of neighborhood networks, of the local community. Even at the most intimate level of sexual relationships, the cultural framework guaranteed a certain stability. Sex was restricted to certain moments of youth, after which it fulfilled only its reproductive purpose and was in any case confined to the couple. Although men still had occasional opportunities for extramarital sex, infidelity among women always constituted a grave breach of the normative order that threatened their very identities.

Today the cultural structure which ensured these equilibria has disintegrated at an astonishing speed. Affective relationships are no longer guaranteed by a stable normative framework and by social support networks; sexuality has become an integral part of love, and the family is no longer the only form of cohabitation between men and women. Relationships between the sexes have become wholly elective and based on personal choice. They thus involve an inherent element of risk, since there is nothing to guarantee the continuity of the relation except the relation itself: whatever it is we do to keep it alive and to nourish it. Uncertainty, therefore, is now irreversibly a component of the relationship between men and women. Their mutual bonds have become far more brittle, and relationships hold or break down according to choices which must be constantly reaffirmed. This, moreover, is true not only of the conjugal relation, but of the broader sphere of relationships between the sexes in general, given the multiplication of occasions for contacts and relations that are not directly oriented towards cohabitation or even sex. Friendship relationships between men and women, too, are made vulnerable by their basis on free choice, and their maintenance requires constant investment. Naturally, the more intense and important the affective charge, the closer we come to love and the more evident and perhaps threatening this vulnerability becomes.

Another factor which today complicates the relationship between the sexes is the pronounced emergence of differences between men and women, and the cultural elaboration of these differences in terms of value, as a cultural consequence above all deriving from the processes of female emancipation and the thrust of the women's movement. Differences that existed also in the past – but which were ordered hierarchically in the cultural (male-dominated) structure and thus effectively kept under control – now burst forth as women forcefully state their own view of the world, claiming cultural legitimation for their perspective. In interpersonal relations, and in particular in love relationships, the enhanced visibility of difference introduces an emotional overload stemming from the new tasks of communication and integration with which the couple must now cope.

Within the couple, the passage from a male monarchy to a basic dyarchy has created an unstable balance of power. In terms of the preconditions of communication, it demands investment in the relationship if it is to be maintained. The richness of difference must be integrated and the potential for conflict contained; upon this achievement, the conditions and the languages of communication must be created and recreated. The relationship between the sexes, especially those between people in love, becomes the domain of labour, a task which requires investments of energy and time. It may establish itself as a factor contributing to still further stress, primarily due to the emotional consequences of uncertainty and on account of the fact that our affective investment in our relationships always overlaps and competes with other times and other demands in our lives. Energy devoted to the 'private' is no less necessary than energy invested in the public sphere, regardless of whether we work actively to achieve equilibrium in our emotional relationships or seek instead to shed their burden. Moreover, our relationships absorb a constant amount of our energies even in times we allow them to exist apparently unthematized. Between the nights we spend in interminable discussions seeking to unravel our differences, and the days we spend in the silence of distance and apparent tranquillity, there is no great difference in terms of emotional investment and stress.

Thus, being a man, being a woman, and living together can no longer be taken for granted. The treasure of the difference and of the encounter must be searched for and unearthed, and we do not always have a map to guide us to the island of dreams. The piercing happiness of successful communication, or the serene tranquillity of everyday gestures accomplished together, are gifts which repay our many labours. Perhaps this is precisely why we never cease to search for them.

However, in terms of their experience of diversity and their relational tasks, men and women are still far from achieving a distribution of duties which, even if not equal, would at least be balanced. The 'work' of the relationship is still mainly the duty of the female. It is as if 'housework' – which is now, at least in part, redistributed between the sexes – has changed its nature. Women still look after the 'household' they share with their men, above all by assuming the burden of the uncertainty and the communicative labours of a relationship that is no longer guaranteed by any external framework.

In achieving recognition, women have affirmed a different outlook on reality, an experience lived in a different body, a specific way of relating with the other and with the world. Either deliberately or implicitly, they bring the *form of communication* into question; they refuse to separate doing from meaning, the action from the emotion that invariably accompanies it. What, moreover, is thereby addressed is the issue of power and difference. Women's experience of masculine power has taught the lesson that difference lends itself to power. Female communication expresses a question and a challenge: whether difference without power is possible, whether communication which preserves the difference is possible.

By anchoring themselves in the female form of communication – which women know remains distinct from male communication but which they have now discovered is also internally differentiated – they interrogate their life within the couple and, hence, within the culture as a whole. At the basic level of communication, they pose the questions of how diversity can be resolved, whether unity in difference can be achieved – in sum, whether communication with the other is possible without imbalance of power. In their relational 'work', women assume responsibility for preserving the particular, the value assigned to the small details of experience, remembrance of the everyday, of small gestures and of times without a history –

activities that have been tritely dismissed as female narcissism when, in fact, they signify a profound cultural transformation. They contradict the standardization of experience and the neutralization of time which male culture requires to succeed in generalizing the procedures of instrumental rationality.

In assuming the task of communication, women engage in a symbolic waste, an apparent lack of effectiveness which contains a profound ambivalence. On the one hand, in fact, they may commit waste in the strict sense of the word: a useless squandering of energy in pursuit of an impossible dream of unity, where the only relational model proposed is the harmony of the maternal womb. The plenitude of the womb, however, hardly corresponds to what is required by a situation of uncertainty, where the risk of individuation and loss defines our lives in a time with few guarantees of relational security. Nevertheless, such symbolic waste by women simultaneously expresses the irreducible difference of that which 'is worthless' as being too minute or too partial to be recognized by male culture. The symbolic dissipation of the energies that women invest in the relation affirms the value of the useless, the absolute right of the particular to exist, the irreducible meaning of inner times – times which no History can record but which make of individual experience the ultimate nucleus of meaning, and of communication the culmination of our experience. The constitutive dichotomy of the feminine, being oneself/being for the other, thus takes new form as a drama and as the symbol of the female in the daily labouring of women to encounter their men.

But neither do the men who have lived through these transformations, nor the generations that come after them, find the task any simpler. As already stated, positive investment in the problem or the attempt to ignore it prove equally costly in emotional terms. The latter is still the typical strategy of men, resorted to in coping with the difficulties of living in togetherness with the difference (even if today we see symptoms of change in this respect). When the habit of masking the difficulties of loving behind silence and neglect is overstretched, male problems explode into the open in more drastic and massive form. Accordingly, men tend to occupy themselves with the difference only in emergencies or when faced by subjectively catastrophic events.

The commonest of these catastrophes are crises in the relationship, often as a result of meeting new partners, of career disappointments or the appearance of marked physical symptoms. These are events that turn the focus of male attention on the relationship, activate a process of self-reflection, and perhaps lay the basis for a new awareness which may even affect the core elements of male culture.

In most cases, separation comes about as a result of new relationships. Another kind of catastrophe is the unexpected appearance of a manifest physical symptom, often of a sexual nature, consequent of a prolonged suppression of the body and the emotions. In both cases, the dynamic nucleus of the catastrophe is a profound injury – not only individual and affective but primarily cultural – to the image of masculine potency. The revelation of their affective, physical, or sexual weakness is an experience that men find difficult to bear but which may also act as a trigger for change.

Although feminism and women's demands for autonomy have profoundly changed at least the outward form of male culture, they have been ambivalent in their effects. Indeed, the postfeminist generations of men often feign weakness as a kind of protective clothing against the threat of real impotence, whether relational or sexual.

This behaviour can also be adapted to deal with the pressures of work life, which undeniably characterize more the experience of male life. Confronted with the risk or the reality of inadequacy, of occupational failure in a society which measures a person's worth by her/his work performance, male culture may resort to a sort of preventive surrender. A cultural model which demands success and major investment in a limited life-phase means that progress can only be gauged in the short term. The experience of failure does not necessarily correspond to objectively sensational events; it may relate to a change of job, to a long sought-after promotion. The perception of failure is often only relative, a subjective judgement deriving from the system of expectations and the cultural pressures to which each individual is exposed. Whatever the case may be, failure or lack of professional success is one of the critical points at which the experience of catastrophe is condensed, and in many cases it may induce men to redefine themselves and to perceive their relationships with their partners under a new light.

An overt physical symptom, a sexual disorder, the threat of illness, or illness itself are sometimes the means by which the magnitude of the affective charge of the relation is disclosed to men. In an external setting where everything is seemingly in order, the body sends out signals of distress. It is more common for women to link a physical symptom directly or indirectly with some aspect of their affective lives or, more generally, their inner psychological world. Male culture, for its part, rather tends to isolate the symptom and more commonly treats it as a problem of physical efficiency. It is more seldom that men locate what is happening to their bodies within the structure of their affective relationships and accept that the problem is not solely a functional one. When, however, they do alter their perspective, the way is opened up for thorough-going personal change.

Today, both men and women confront the abyss of difference, and what I have termed 'male' and 'female' does not correspond to gender in the biological sense alone. On the one hand, the models of male culture still exert their pressure on women who have won their freedom; on the other, cultural change has induced and enabled many men to begin a profound redefinition of themselves. For men and women alike, the possibility of communication is mediated by passion for the encounter and respect for the limit.

Culture as difference

What I have described so far at the individual level is part of collective changes spreading all over the world. When social relations multiply and intersect at a growing pace, difference is increasingly met at the cultural level. In a global society conflicts based on culture, ethnicity and nation are important signs of the changing role of identity and of the appeal of difference. This, however, is not their only meaning and many different levels coexist within the same historical phenomena, which should never be considered as unified realities, particularly in their more visible political dimensions.

In terms of *orientations* of action, ethnicity or cultural difference can provide a criterion along which to organize the defence of material interests of a group against discrimination, marginalization, or exploitation. In other cases, ethnicity can be a channel through which people express their demands for new rights and try to define a political space for excluded social groups. Besides material or political goals, ethnic and cultural identification can also play the role of a symbolic and selective resource answering the challenges of identity in a complex society: legacy of ethnic and cultural traditions provides a ready answer to the critical question of identity. It offers, particularly to the young generations, the opportunity to reinterpret in a selective way the cultural material of the tradition, in order to answer new questions or to resist the pressures imposed by a global society.

Other analytical distinctions among different forms of ethnic and cultural conflicts concern their social and political *contexts*. At least four different dimensions should be separated. Ethnic problems can be related to the global migration processes, the interdependence and the imbalances of the world labour market, and the reactions of the host societies. Secondly, ethnic problems can be related to the pluralism of groups of relatively equal size within the borders of a nation state. A third dimension has to do with interstate conflicts when the same ethnic or cultural group lives on two sides of the same border. And finally, ethnic claims for autonomy or independence by minority groups can be addressed to a relatively homogeneous nation state for the purpose of achieving the political control over a given territory.

A third level of analysis concerns the *meaning* of ethnic and cultural action, which can vary from defence and resistance against modernization processes to demands for political rights, to a challenge to the international system, which remains in fact an interstate system. Conflicts that mobilize ethnic and cultural identities make visible the crisis of the nationstate and bring to the fore the need for a new transnational world system capable of recognizing and integrating differences. The nationstates are losing their authority as, towards the top of the system, planetary interdependence and the emergence of transnational political and economic forces shift the actual locus of decision-making elsewhere, while, towards the bottom, the proliferation of autonomous decision-making centres endows 'civil societies' with a specific power.

An articulated set of conceptual tools can help us to differentiate the many levels of ethnic and cultural conflicts which too often are treated as homogeneous. Such an analysis makes it easier to understand that these conflicts, together with the old problems of economic discrimination and marginalization and with the claims to political autonomy and recognition, bring to the surface new problems. They address the redefinition of a world system based on international relations; a system formally organized on the relations among sovereign states, but in fact governed by the North–South imbalances, by central and regional powers, by the lack of a global responsibility. These conflicts make clear the necessity of a different global organisation of political issues.

But they also raise another important challenge, the right to name the world in a specific way. Every ethnic or traditional culture speaks its own language and tries to have its right to do so. Besides the political aspect of recognition, there is a deeper importance of this issue. Culture is increasingly shaped by anonymous apparatuses imposing the names and the languages through which people should understand and relate to reality. Naming the world in a different way challenges this homogenization and the imposition of standardized codes. In this respect ethnic and cultural conflicts join other recent forms of collective action, challenging the new powers telling people how they should name reality (personal and gender relations, relation to nature, health, sexuality, birth and death, consumption).

Difference and ethics

Dealing with these critical issues calls for nothing less than a new moral attitude. A term that I have already introduced summarizes the ethical implications of what was presented here. 'Metamorphosis' comes from the Greek and literally means to change form or to overcome one's form. The expression of differences goes together with the need for communication and solidarity. But in order to meet otherness, one needs to change form. We cannot communicate or relate to differences by simply remaining ourselves. In the issue of multi-culturalism, which implies some capacity and will to meet the 'other', there is a profound moral implication: the necessity to keep and to lose, to cope with fears and resistances, but also with the ability of going beyond our given identities.

There is therefore a necessity to deal with ambivalence, because neither the dominant nor the dominated are free from ambivalent feeling towards the 'other'. The possibility of meeting each other needs a big leap in consciousness, to allow people to accept that they exist as separate individuals and social groups, but no less that they can *co*-exist and communicate. To take responsibility for one's own identity means also to accept one's limits and to open up to the other through negotiated, ongoing partnership.

Misunderstandings are part of the present situation in political, scientific, and everyday exchanges. We have to take responsibility for our misunderstandings, whose permanent sources are differences of languages, of frameworks, of values. We have, first, to acknowledge and not just condemn them, in order to start communicating about them. Trying to make our starting point as clear as possible and trying to listen to the other person or group as much as possible, are ways to overcome the simple expression of differences. We should not believe that difference in itself, and difference alone, could be a value. Difference is just one side of human relations. Community, solidarity, communication are the other side. When difference alone becomes a banner, the results can be paradoxical and, more often, violent. Unfortunately, the extreme stress on differences is far more serious and it can bring in dramatic forms of fundamentalism and violence. The problem is never just difference, but rather the parallel necessity to overcome it, to make the constant effort of listening and understanding each other.

8

Amorous senses

Loving and reproducing

Sexuality without reproduction and reproduction without sexuality combined bring to the fore the radically contingent nature of love relationships and reveal otherness as the immutable condition of 'being with'. The societies in which we live increasingly intervene in their own reproduction. First and foremost the biological basis of human behaviour becomes a target for social intervention and manipulation, with human reproduction itself emerging as a prime object of such interference. Consequentially, reproduction ceases to be a destiny and is finally transformed into a field of decision, action, and choice. But whose choice? Of individuals responsible for their own existence and thus presumably capable of deciding, or at least deciding whether to decide? Or of scientific, medical, and social apparatuses which fix the codes of behaviour, the canons of normality and of pathology?

The fact that reproduction is *de facto* no longer preordained introduces an aspect of a new and radical ambivalence into our cultural life. While the growth of information, medical progress, and changing morals and sexual customs offer men and women a new range of reproductive choices as well as responsibilities, the external control of their behaviour simultaneously increases. Such control is exercised not just through the manifest action of repressive apparatuses or authoritarian norms; it also operates through symbolic codes which govern our behavior and via the manipulation of the bio-psychological bases of human action.

In contemporary societies the reproduction of the human species has thus ceased to be a fact of nature. Suspended between biology and culture, the reproductive domain has always constituted the point of contact between the biological blueprint and our species' ability to produce meanings and social relations. Even adaptation of the human society to the environment – a crucial factor in our reproductive destiny – has always taken the form of an encounter between nature and the capacity for cultural elaboration.

However, on the threshold of the twenty-first century, reproduction seems to have been stripped of even the last of its remaining natural roots and entirely converted into a social commodity. While reproduction above all ensures the biological continuation of the species, the profound change in its 'natural' status is marked symbolically by two phenomena which radically undermine the 'naturalness' of human evolution: the threat of nuclear war and the manipulation of the genetic code. Both of these phenomena signal an irreversible shift in the direction of the species' evolutionary future: they tell us that our survival no longer depends on our reproductive capacity but rather on the choices we make between destruction, conservation, or transformation – for both ourselves and other living species. Considering, then, that these phenomena now have acquired a dimension that is planetary in its scope – that is, they embrace the species as a whole and the entire ecosystem – it becomes obvious that 'nature' has irrevocably lost its role in the evolutionary destiny of mankind and of the planet as something that escapes human intervention.

As regards reproduction in particular, the process that most evidently manifests this change is the marked divarication of sexuality and reproduction. In the history of the species, the distinction between these two levels has had the effect of a powerful generator of culture; what has been written, imagined, and created on the subject of love testifies to the possibility of conceiving and giving symbolic form to the separation between eros and reproductive necessity.

However, this possibility always represented an exception, or at least was the privilege of restricted social groups only. Only with the social transformations of the last few decades has the split between sexuality and reproduction become a phenomenon that reflects wider reality of mass dimensions and an accomplished cultural fact. Two processes have been decisive in this regard. First, advances in medical-biological knowledge now make it technically possible to intervene in our reproductive mechanism. Second, cultural changes have profoundly altered the familial and reproductive role of women and the sexuality of young people.

The possibility of direct control of reproduction has evolved through a rapid succession of scientific discoveries, proliferation of pharmacological experiments, and the development of medical techniques. The social acceptance and diffusion of the products of these processes, again, has been helped by a changed cultural climate and by the emergence of new attitudes, especially so among young people and women.

The sexual behaviour of the young people has undergone transformations in close correspondence with the rise of an independent youth culture freed from the constraints of the adult world. Sexual experience is acquired increasingly earlier and has expanded its inherent meanings, so that it now represents a stage in youthful initiation and grants access to the culture of the group. Sex is predominantly communicative and socializing in its purpose, while its reproductive function has virtually disappeared.

In a different way, the new culture of women has also profoundly affected the meaning of sexuality. Traditionally denied, or tolerated as a price to be paid for the imperative of motherhood, female sexuality has acquired its autonomy as a new consciousness has arisen among women. When women reject their subordinate position along with the rigidity of familial roles which bind them to their destinies as mothers and wives, they, or at least their younger generation, can begin to choose the sexuality they prefer: as a source of pleasure, as an instrument of communication, or as eros unconstrained by reproduction.

Cognitive and technical resources, changes in cultural models and relational patterns have thus irreversibly severed sexuality from its association with reproduction. Symbolically and in actual practice, the two most striking examples of this split are represented by contraception and artificial insemination: sexuality without reproduction in the first case, reproduction without sexuality in the second. When contraception is practised on a mass scale, the separation between the sexual act and its reproductive purpose is completed: human sexuality becomes a field of experience open to the possible, an area of symbolic investment where meaning is defined by the partners themselves. The techniques of artificial conception developed over the last few decades represent the other half of the separation between sexuality and reproduction: for the first time ever, the reproduction once 'naturally' ordained as impossible can take place independently of the sexual encounter between the parents.

Whether we interpret the necessary link between sexuality and reproduction that has characterized the evolution of the species as a trick of nature or as a divine plan, the realization that it is now irreversibly cut off comes as an astounding experience. The future of the species (reproduction) and love between men and women (sexuality) seem to lose that solid anchorage the two used to provide for each other. By whom and how can the continuation of our species be guaranteed, if reproduction becomes only one possible option among several? Again, what kind of reproduction are we to choose among the many alternatives available now that the natural 'constraint' of sexuality has been lifted?

On the other hand, on the side of sexuality, what is the future of an eros untrammelled by reproductive necessity, freed from constraints, from dangers, but also from the responsibilities of its biological purpose? What may love become when it is separated from reproduction and from the sexual encounter between men and women? How and where exactly can we make room for the erotic 'creation' that may well replace procreation?

Life-choices

Just as in other areas of life, so in the sexual and reproductive sphere the range of possibilities expands. The cultural and technical options available allow everyone the chance to select and to locate her/his own self. In an area where the univocal and linear character of 'natural' processes disappears, sexual and reproductive choice becomes individualized and escapes the regular patterning of a general model.

The sphere of sexuality and reproduction resembles an enormous laboratory where a wide variety of cultural models are experimented with and put into practice. This pluralization is most evident in intracouple relationships. The heterosexual and monogamous couple – the cornerstone of the institution of the modern family and the guarantor of the continuation of the reproductive process – is now flanked by new, parallel models which coexist with it and have even become institutionalized: homosexual couples, 'singles', and all the other *ad hoc* arrangements between partners living together outside a stable matrimonial relationship.

In the field of reproduction, for the first time ever it is now possible to reverse, and in a certain sense to switch, the two poles of the reproductive process: fertility and sterility. With contraception and sterilization on the one hand, and artificial fertilization on the other, fertility and sterility too have lost their status as destinies allotted by nature. Consequently, we are now able to transform into alternative options what once used to constitute a necessary polarity between two opposed and mutually exclusive conditions.

One of the many paradoxes of our age is that research, experimentation, and campaigning focusing on birth control and sterilization proceed simultaneously with the spread of increasingly sophisticated techniques of artificial fertilization.

In this manner, the dimension of choice reaches a paramount position. It invades and occupies our entire experiential field of sexuality and reproduction. When speaking of choice, however, we must recognize that alongside it, we also have a capacity for intervention. We possess, that is, a threefold power over sexuality, reproduction, and birth.

Intervention in sexuality mostly assumes the form of the medicalization of sexuality and birth control. As the object of scientific observation and analysis, sexuality has now definitively entered the scientific domain. New definitions and rules of sexual conduct pour forth, and the media offer a plethora of sexual guidance and counselling. Sexology, as a branch of medicine and psychotherapy, has grown and attained its legitimation on this basis. Simultaneously, contraception and sterilization have become common in broad sections of the population, while abortion has established itself as an institutionalized method for reducing the birth rate, applied, however, always reflecting quantitative and qualitative control.

As regards reproduction, artificial fertilization is today possible using a variety of methods ranging from artificial insemination to *in vitro* fertilization. The options available cover almost every possible combination of the variables that govern reproduction: maternal egg/egg from a female donor; paternal sperm/sperm from a male donor; sterile mother/sterile father; a maternal uterus able/unable to bring pregnancy to its conclusion.

Social intervention in birth is also increasingly common. The medicalization of childbirth seems now to be an irreversible process. Even those who have attempted to humanize it, especially the women's movement, seem to unquestioningly accept the guarantees of safety and the control of emergencies provided by the hospital maternity ward. Thus ever greater numbers of children are given birth in hospitals, and there is a simultaneous increase in information and counselling services for their parents, being directed at both the actual birth and the subsequent care of the child. As a result of the advances in embryological and perinatal research, as well as in the techniques of prior intervention in intra-uterine life, another area of social intervention now concentrates on the fetus.

These closely interacting processes have written a new chapter in the history of human societies – that of reproduction by choice – but they also demonstrate the intrinsic ambivalence of the concept of 'choice'; it embraces both our decisions and the interventions by institutions, apparatuses, and organizations. Whose choice is it, then?

On the one hand, it undoubtedly remains ours. We are better informed about our bodies and our sexuality; we enjoy greater freedom in our choice of partner; we are better protected against the risks associated with the 'natural' dimension of sexuality (unpredictability, pathologies, emergencies); and we are more adept at choosing among the multiple options – even in terms of ethics – availed to us in the uncoupling of eros from reproduction.

On the other hand, however, choice is to an equal degree exercised by the apparatuses and institutions that intervene in the sexual and reproductive sphere by making technical decisions and establishing procedures which, even if they appear 'neutral', nevertheless establish symbolic control over the field. Information is monopolized, and our relationships are manipulated by the numerous forms of counselling now on offer, by the screening function of the systems of expertise to which we are forced to resort, and by the careful monitoring of broad sections of the population by medical apparatuses (prevention policies, imposition of risk categories).

Reproduction remains fundamentally a matter of choice. Yet it is profoundly ambivalent and exposed to the risk of unforeseen circumstances, new power arrangements, and new conflicts. In particular, artificial fertilization techniques already foreshadow the end of paternity and maternity as biological events, and weaken the last buttress of natural childbearing, that of *mater certa*. The use of a donor's ovum or uterus has undermined the principle, raising intricate legal issues and calling the only biological foundation of our identity into question. This introduces the real possibility of gestation outside the body to match the extracorporeal conception that artificial insemination and *in vitro* fertilization have already made possible. This radical change in filial relationships will remove any natural connotation from paternity and maternity, so that life-giving and child-rearing become purely matters of cultural choice, open to a wide range of meanings.

We may thus already imagine social control extending to include even our innermost drives and needs, as policies regarding reproduction inevitably penetrate to the deepest levels of affective life.

Sexuality, eros, and gratuitousness

We have, then, arrived at a situation in which love is progressively detached from the reproductive drive and is establishing itself as a sheer matter of choice. In this process, love becomes the domain of possible communication, of the gratuitous encounter with the other. No longer tied to reproduction, sexuality may now become an encounter mediated by our bodies and releasing the most intimate of our spiritual energies. The Tantric and Taoist culture of the East has always viewed sex in this way – as an experience initiating restricted elites into a higher knowledge. Today this possibility is making itself more and more felt in Western culture as well. Yet, such an experience of sexuality as a gift, as a quest for the self and for the other, is an option that remains vulnerable to tendencies drawing it to directions quite opposite to its promise.

Sexuality without reproduction may turn into sexuality without eros. In a culture where performance counts everything, sex is stripped of its erotic force and reduced to mere gymnastics of the orgasm. The medical and scientific vulgarization of sexuality has established models of efficiency and set standards of behaviour which sanction the criteria and requisites for a 'satisfactory sex life'. In the cultural models broadcast by the media and by the market, the body appears as nothing more than a machine for sexual display. We are inundated by sexual stimuli (above all visual), but this glut of messages removes the erotic content from sex and leaves only the genitalia. The effect of sexuality displayed but de-eroticized is the neutralization of desire.

At the psychological level, anxiety and insecurity over sexual matters increase, while erotic tension, the deep mainspring of the relationship, slackens and loses its force. The fragility of the psychic structure is exacerbated by the stress factors present in the environment: competition and conflicts in the workplace, the pace of urban life and its pollution, dietary imbalances and the chemical adulteration of food. The waning of desire, the impoverishment of the imagination, do not reveal to us the roots of the process; they instead impel us to search for new stimuli and to intensify bodily display. This, then, further debases sexuality already transforming into mere genital performance, eliminating the last chance to reappropriate the body as a vehicle to express love. Pornography draws on this impoverishment, transforms it into a commodity for legal and illegal markets, and fills with fictive sensations the lack of satisfactory and passionate sexual relationships.

Sexual difficulties thus become another component in the relationships between the sexes, in addition to those examined in the previous chapter. Sterility and sexual disorders are increasingly common – signals to which men and women respond in different ways. The perception of a disorder by men often goes nowhere beyond its symptom, thus precluding any redefinition of the problem that moves from the physical signal to the person as a whole and, above all, to the relation. Women's relationships with their bodies are governed by a set of biological constants: the menstrual cycle and motherhood, always confronted at least as a desire or a refusal. In female experience, the presence of these constants acts as a kind of permanent signalling by the body, even in those cases where individual sensitivity to the bodily dimension has decreased. Men, instead, more commonly neutralize the messages emitted by the body or interpret them purely symptomatically. An alternative masculine reaction is to seek to increase their bodily efficiency by means of sport or physical exercise. It is thus more often the women who assume the burden of the love relationship and its difficulties by manifesting physical and sexual distress.

Men and women also contend, through their sexual difficulties, with the most general imperatives of our culture, which we may plot along the axes of strength/weakness, speed/standstill, efficiency/uselessness. The experience of our weakness intimidates us and brings into question our very identity. Our self-realization and our ability to leave our mark on the world depend on whether or not we can keep pace with the rhythm of change. Should we fall behind or if we come to a halt, we risk exclusion. Likewise, if we are unable to keep pace with external demands and fail to meet performance standards, we are invaded by a feeling of uselessness. Precisely because of the importance attributed to sexuality in our culture, sexual difficulties become the gauge and the stigma of male and female inadequacy. Backtracking here from the signal to the content of the message is no easy job, but it is nevertheless the only route to the realization that nothing is ever solely a question of sex.

For consideration of the risks and obstacles of a sexuality no longer tied to reproduction once again raises the problem of choice. The weakening of external guarantees and the decline of the ideal of romantic love mean that choice provides the only foundation for the love relationship. Yet it, alone, accentuates the dimension of gratuitousness in the encounter, since by itself it is unable to issue guarantees of permanence through time, while nothing ensures that it can be repeated with a similar outcome in moments of difficulty. It is within the relationship itself that the partners must look for their reasons for choice, even when obstacles impede it. Without predictability and without continuity, love cannot survive, and what we need is a pact, if possible a negotiated and reversible one. But if the foundation of love is now given in the act of choice, and that only, then with every difficulty and every estrangement from the other we revert to the choice and call the pact into question.

It seems, therefore, that love must inevitably pass beyond the pact and continue its search for a foundation elsewhere. Here *gratuitousness*, the sense of something freely bestowed or obtained, granted or provided without expectation or reward, creates a new spiritual dimension for us. It leads us to the part of ourselves that many traditions of the past identified as the creative force of eros – a force which extends beyond our immediate relationships and places us in relation with the cosmos. Eros freed from reproductive obligations can assist us in finding new forms of language to name love and to reformulate in worldly terms our need to overcome otherness and to respect its limit. Love, as a pure choice and acceptance of the other, as the grateful recognition of another person's existence, needs a new spiritual foundation to give to the mundane relationships a breath of infinity and to help to simultaneously accept and overcome their unavoidable limits. Religious language, which used to provide such a foundation through notions like 'divine love' or 'universal love', seems increasingly unable to support the emerging needs with meaningful answers. The search for a mundane foundation of love as the capacity to 'surrender' to otherness and to worship it becomes a new cultural challenge for interpersonal relations as well as for mankind as a whole.

In the immediate environment of everyday experience, apart from relationships with partners, the contingent nature of love also affects the relations with children. When biological filiation eludes the necessity of nature, the parent–child relationship too becomes based on the gratuitousness of choice. This brings about a profound change in adult–infant relationships. Children are no longer the biological continuation of their parents they once represented, nor are they purely objects of breeding and rearing, the receptacles into which we deposit the values and norms of society. They are now both individuals endowed with personal autonomy and partners in a love relationship; partners, moreover, from whom we may still learn the wonder of the play and of unanswerable questions.

The relation with children which will increasingly lose its biological foundation, becomes then a metaphor for any love relationship where unconditioned choice and acceptance are the only 'good reasons' for being together.

9

Inhabiting the earth

Questions without answers

The discourse of nature that by now invades every aspect of our daily lives both emphasizes and conceals the dilemmas of complexity. Yet, in spite of the fashionable status to which ecology has ascended along with the exploitation of environmental issues to market everything from cars to baby food, the very remarkability of the phenomenon reveals behind itself more than meets the eye. The environmental debate is a symptom, a signal which on closer inspection discloses the existence of something else. What, then, does it have to say to the inhabitants of a planet which today is the home of a global society?

It certainly tells us about the great dilemmas which today characterize our lives: we cannot choose between nature and technology; we try to abide by the rules of 'environmental correctedness' but we cannot reduce our consumption standards; we all are potential NIMBYs ('not in my back-yard') when our immediate environment is concerned.

Uncertainty grows on a par with the increasing complexity of the systems in which we inextricably live, and decisions are responses through which we seek to reduce the degree of uncertainty present in our fields of action. Decision-making – the process which enables us to take action – is, however, also an attempted evasion, a denial and a concealment of the dilemmas that lie beneath the decision itself.

Today we are confronted with unresolvable problems which define the cultural and social confines of complexity, each putting us face to face with an impossible alternative of having to choose between polar oppositions. For it is precisely the tension between the twin poles of these problems that forms the thread on which the unstable equilibrium of the planetary system rests and renews itself. None the less, they are problems we must inevitably seek to resolve, even when the act of their apparent solution accomplishes nothing but a shift of the uncertainty elsewhere. The method through which we attempt to deal with these problems, then, is decision-making. But the decisions also constitute for us ways through which we seek to avoid the tension at times growing near-unbearable, by glossing over our dilemmas and by refusing to call them by their name.

The foremost of these dilemmas is that between *autonomy* and *control*; between, on the one hand, the need to valorize individual skills and choices and, on the other, our tendency to create tightly-knit systems of behavioural manipulation which today stand ready to govern our brains and our biological structure itself. Nuclear power and genetic engineering testify in different ways to our society's extreme capacity to generate itself to the point of full control of its own life-conditions, including for the first time ever the capability also of their negation at will: total self-destruction. This in turn creates a further dilemma between *responsibility* and *omnipotence*, between the drive to increase the capacity of human systems for self-intervention and the need to respond to the constraints imposed by nature within and without ourselves.

Closely linked with this dilemma is a third one. The action that our species takes on itself and on its environment is regulated by irreversible scientific knowledge which cannot be erased (except under the hypothetical if not unrealistic scenario of a regressive catastrophe obliterating the present evolutionary stage of humankind). At the same time, however, our ability to use this knowledge depends on reversible choices regarding energy, scientific, and military policies, and the behaviour of the apparatuses that govern these choices. Here a dilemma arises between the *irreversibility of knowledge* and the *reversibility of choices,* having dramatic repercussions for the reflection on the prospects for a public ethic in the postnuclear age.

Finally, the planetary extension of the world system has by now acquired a total scope: countries and cultures only exist as inner dimensions of the global system. This new 'internalization' introduces a fourth dilemma, that between *inclusion* and *exclusion*. Inclusion irons out differences and transforms peripheral cultures into insignificant and quaint appendages to the few centres where languages are elaborated and diffused through the great market of the media. Any resistance to this standardization almost inevitably leads to exclusion, spelling silence and cultural death.

Almost never directly named, these great dilemmas nevertheless overshadow the decisions by which we seek to resume governance over complexity. The bland neutrality of procedures serves to mask, and thus to remove from debate and control, many of the issues bearing directly on the lives of each one of us, the destiny of the species, and the directions of its future evolution. Today, in order to bring these dilemmas to light, extra awareness and action is required of us, since it is by means of these qualities that we may redefine the notion of liberty handed down to us from the modern age.

In postmaterial societies, where primary needs can now be fully satisfied, freedom *from* need is replaced by the freedom *of* need, involving the awareness that needs depend on choice, that they are not necessities imposed by scarcity. The cultural dimension of needs becomes paramount and opens up the unpredictable realm of project, of creation, of gratuitousness. The freedom to *have* enjoyed by *homo oeconomicus* has now been replaced by the freedom to *be*. The fact again provokes a conflict between the new powers which intervene in birth and death, health and sickness, our biological and sexual natures, and on the other side the need to take control of our existence and decide its quality. From the right to *equality* – the watchword of the modern revolutions but still far from an accomplished fact – stems today's right to *difference*. Recognizing and granting the right of people, languages, and cultures to be different opens up the way for a new definition of solidarity and communal life.

The world in which we live still has far to go before these rights are guaranteed, especially in view of the cleavages persisting among geopolitical blocs, the almost unbridgeable divide between North and South, and the mounting crescendo of rage among the dispossessed. Yet these rights do unquestionably exist, and are now being extended to shape our daily lives and civil culture as well. On them depends our ability to adopt a new perspective in confronting the great dilemmas of our time, even those planetary problems which seem so dramatically insoluble.

Confrontation over these rights extends well beyond the dangers of pollution to constitute a new culture of the species. Human time and space are by now inextricably entwined in the awareness that we form a part of the planet and the universe beyond. Mankind must assume responsibility for inhabiting the earth and for setting unbreachable confines on the destructive production of the species; human culture must learn to circumscribe again the territory where silence and respect are due to whatever exists purely because it exists. Every human society has recognized such a territory in its own way, and societies with the acquired power to create and destroy themselves must now redefine it for themselves. Life on planet Earth is no longer guaranteed by a divine order; it now rests in the weak and fumbling hands of us all.

Limit and possibility

The implication of this last statement is that our action must be defined as the construction of the possibilities within the given-perceived limits. I employ the term 'limit' here in two senses. 'Limit' first denotes finiteness, the recognition that corporeality and death are the space of our condition. The body that lives, suffers, and dies interrogates our faith in technology – which has replaced the relationship with the sacred of other cultures – as a persistent reminder of the fact that human time is only and always provisional.

Limit, however, also stands for confinement, frontier, separation; it therefore also signifies recognition of the other, the different, the irreducible. The encounter with otherness is an experience that puts us to a test: from it is born the temptation to reduce difference by force, while it may equally generate the challenge of communication, as a constantly renewed endeavour.

The emphasis on possibility, on the other hand, signals, first, our uncontainable urge to overcome the limit of pain and death, to push further the spatial and temporal confines of human experience. Second, it testifies to our species' tendency to cerebralize the body and to 'elevate' it to the realm of meaning produced by the higher faculties. Although we ourselves are nature, we are caught in a constant search for and creation of meaning for that nature. Finally, the emphasis on possibility reminds us of the dimension of solidarity and of communication, as the impulse to render diversity less opaque and less irreducible. The 'other' is not just a limit for us, but also a possibility of discovering through difference that we can communicate and reach communality on a higher level.

The tension between limits and possibilities affects in particular the conception of rationality as defined in the modern West. While the deceptive character of a rationality that is based exclusively on calculation of means and ends becomes increasingly evident, the way is opened for new forms of knowledge to arise. Emotions, intuition, creativity, and the 'female' perception of the world become fully incorporated into the process by which our individual and social reality is constructed. Today, instead of disregarding the role of these forms of consciousness, we must grant them recognition.

Similarly, ethical capacity loses the certainty of absolute ends and finds itself consigned to the responsibility and the risk of *co*-living amongst the difference. As the divisions between our planet's regions and peoples grow more acute every hour, responsibility increasingly shifts its locus towards individual action. The survival of the ecosystem depends on our ability to choose consciously. For this reason, the inner planet becomes of such critical concern to us: as that which most intimately defines us and belongs to us, and as our link and access route to the rest of the universe. It is also by developing our capacity of being individuals in relation that we can contribute to a new and shared responsibility towards the planet and mankind.

Living and living-with

As human relations no longer are guaranteed by biological necessity or the inevitability of historical laws, they undergo transformation into a field of choice, into a realm of uncertainty and risk. Communication, the arena of responsibility as the capacity to respond to the other and to ourselves, brings the different into contact. The gratuitousness of the encounter as a gift and reciprocity passes beyond interpersonal relations to encompass our relationship with the planet and the cosmos.

But far from depicting a transparent society of eros, creativity, and expression, this perspective accentuates the ambivalence of our behaviour; an ambivalence which rests entirely on the paradox of human sociability. The order of the gratuitous, of the non-calculable, testifies to the irreducibility of the individual to the relation, of one to two; simultaneously, however, it reveals our deep-rooted need to *live with*.

When human relations are almost entirely governed by choice, the foundation of solidarity is undermined and the social bond is dangerously weakened. From now on, the threat of societal breakdown and of catastrophic individualism will forever loom on the horizon.

However, if we accept that not everything in our relationships is entirely calculable and that not everything can be accounted for by exchange, then the irreducible otherness that characterizes the experience of every individual provides the basis for a new freedom and nourishes solidarity with a discriminating (not blind) passion. This conscious fragility is the starting-point of a change in the ethical attitudes that can underpin social solidarity.

We need an ethic that does not insulate us against the risk of choice and which enables us to metacommunicate about the goals of choice and the criteria that underlie the decision. Such an ethic emerges as irreducibly situational, as an ethic that preserves the dignity of the individual decision and forges anew the bonds that bind us to the species, to living beings, to the cosmos – an ethic, in short, which preserves our ability to wonder at reality without interrupting our capacity to change form.

Discovering that salvation is no longer guaranteed by any final destiny of history demolishes Western rationality with its pretensions to absolute-ness and its will to domination. Simultaneously, however, this rationality is resurrected as an aspiration to a human life endowed with sense, as the rea-sonableness of co-living and as the experience of finiteness. If values are no longer absolute, then their only foundation can be mankind's ability to reach agreement.

Stretched between the two poles which mark the confines of the human condition, removed from nature by our capacity for language and restored to it through our bodies, we must look to language and to the body as the foundations of an ethic responding to the need to cope with the problems of a planet by now wholly shaped by our intervening action.

The body maps the confines of nature within and without us: the great rhythms of birth and death, the permanent cycle of day and night, of the seasons, of growth and aging. In a world that technology has constructed, equilibrium, rhythm, and respect for limits are no longer – if they ever were – the spontaneous outcome of a nature as 'mother and mentor'. Rather, they are the fruits of individual and collective choices, of a conscious morality which both assumes *responsibility for* and *responds to* nature.

It is precisely this dual significance of responsibility that roots ethics in language. Culture is the realm in which every moral choice must necessar-ily take shape. In our planetary society of information, to name is to bring into existence. The simplistic idea that information mirrors a 'reality in itself' is a residue from the past whose authority we must renounce. Information *is* reality – if only because our experience is by now entirely *mediated* by the representations and the images that we produce. Nature, as the foundation that grounds the experience and as the external reality that grounded the question of truth and falsehood has ceased to exist inde-pendently of the effects of social intervention. Culture becomes the space where reality will be defined and Nature itself preserved or destroyed.

What, then, is to be done with language – this is the new frontier of an ethics of complexity. How and for what purpose should we use the *power of naming* which allows us to fabricate the world and to subsume it to the signs with which we express (or do not express) it?

Power does not only lie outside us as a threat to be exorcised. If instead of projecting it externally we realize that it is a relation, then it becomes constitutive of all our relationships while still remaining in our own posses-sion. It is language which takes up the challenge of creation of meaning or its reduction to signs. Through empty or meaningful words, words which hide or which reveal, it is within language that nature can be erased or brought to existence.

We must therefore learn to move between body and language – or rather between the different languages which we use to nominate our world – flexibly, willing to accept change, and respectful of the limit. The criteria and values guiding our choices are no longer supported by any stable underpinning; today we can only *produce together* our world, recognizing its constructed character and its temporal confines. For individuals and the collectivity alike, this entails accepting that our *existence is temporary* and that *we can change*. This reintroduces the theme of metamorphosis, of the capacity to change form, as a condition for societal living.

A choice of this kind will weave back together all the threads that tie us to the species, to all living beings, and to the cosmos. Each of us may then recognize her/his own responsibility for the destiny of humankind and for future generations, regaining thereby the lost respect for other species and for the universe of which mankind is part. Such recognition distills all the wisdom that traditional cultures have handed down to the technological culture of complex systems into a single, fundamental legacy: that we can continue to wonder at that which exists.

10

A eulogy to wonder

Smiling, laughing, and other pleasantries

Laughter is a very serious subject indeed. Since Freud, it has occupied the energies of the most earnest of scholars, and learned books and treatises on it abound. We know, however, that what happens in laughter cannot be fully captured by the talk of it, and that talking about laughter will not make us laugh. Nevertheless, we need to venture into a discussion of this special dimension of our everyday experience, for without it everything I have said so far loses in significance. Laughter, so familiar and accessible an event to us all, brings us most directly into contact with the experience of the limit and of possibility.

Humans are the only animals capable of laughter. Other species solve problems and are even able to learn languages, yet they are unable to laugh. Only humans laugh, and, at the present stage of our evolutionary progress, laughter apparently represents an innate form of behaviour: a baby first smiles after five or six weeks of life and then begins to laugh between the fifth and sixth month. Laughter certainly serves to express emotions, to communicate, to facilitate encountering others. After the triumph of *homo faber* and the subsequent discovery of his limitations, the time has perhaps arrived for us to concern ourselves with *homo ridens*.

The act of laughter involves complex processes, both physiological and psychological, which require no analysis when we laugh – the experience of laughter is always an integral one. It comes about above all as a physical experience, muscular and respiratory. When we laugh the face grows round, the facial muscles are flexed, the skin stretches, the eyebrows are raised to form an arch, the eyes glisten, the corners of the mouth are lifted and pulled backwards, the furrow in the upper lip deepens, the nostrils flare. Simultaneously, our breathing and heartbeat both accelerate. This complex set of physiological processes has perplexed researchers studying the evolutionary roots of laughter in our species' history. The phylogenetic hypothesis is that laughter originated as a reaction to situations of conflict, leaving some of its integral features behind (heavy breathing, the jerky movement of the limbs, the facial mimicry and, especially, the display of the teeth). The first act of laughter was a snarl which acquired symbolic significance as a yell of triumph, an exultation and a sudden release of tension. Alternatively, laughter has been interpreted as a signal that danger has passed or been averted, thus performing a more explicitly communicative function within the group. Thus, in phylogenetic terms, these hypotheses suggest a close psychological connection between laughter and aggression, laughter and fear, and, ultimately, laughter and weeping. They establish, that is, a relationship between laughter and a dimension of menace or potential suffering. Animal behaviour comprises a series of postures, grimaces, and wrinkling of the snout which, although resembling the physical manifestation of laughter, are in fact fear responses. Children's games often mix fear and laughter together: for instance, a child pretending to be chased will cry and giggle at the same time.

The most important physiological feature of laughter is the movement of the thorax. When we laugh, the muscles of the chest alternately expand and relax, with a marked effect on respiration. The hyperventilation of the lungs and the increased oxygenation of the blood produce the feeling of well-being that typically accompanies laughter. This activity steps up the production of hormones – adrenaline, noradrenaline, and dopamine – which trigger the release of endorphins: natural morphines with a tranquillizing effect that reinforce our immunity system. The process is an abrupt one; its onset is sudden, it lasts only a few moments, and its termination is equally quick. It is the brevity of laughter that distinguishes it from happiness: the one is a short-lived bodily event, the other a background state which persists over time. Studies on drugs, especially marijuana and LSD, have shown that these substances impact on the same neurotransmitters as those that laughter activates – a fact which has led various writers to describe laughter as a natural drug or medicine.

When we laugh, the experience is immediate, brief, and intense; it begins and then it quickly comes to an end. Laughter is an explosion, and while we laugh we are largely unaware of what is happening to us. If we monitor our behaviour carefully, however, we note a subjective sensation of enormous warmth and a generalized sense of well-being. Indeed, the popular truism that 'laughter is the best medicine' is thus borne out by contemporary research. Laughter releases in our bodies various substances which activate health-promoting circuits of regeneration and defence. The problem, though, is that we cannot command ourselves to laugh. Laughter is essentially spontaneous; it is an unexpected and unpredictable phenomenon. Even when we have dissected and analyzed its physiological, psychological, and cultural mechanisms, we still remain unable to produce laughter mechanically through rational thought or an act of will.

Laughter is an immediate and primary experience; an event of the body which encompasses both psychology and culture and which is therefore entirely human. Analyzing its processes does not, and cannot, evoke laughter; nevertheless it may help us to understand how we laugh and what makes us laugh.

How we laugh

We are now at an appropriate point to distinguish between the major categories of the overall experience of laughter. Its main forms are humour, irony, satire, and comedy, which is usually taken to be the general category which embraces all the others. Humour is a way of laughing *with* other people. It requires a proper time and place, as well as a special language shared by the interlocutors, and it usually acts as a safety valve for the tensions provoked by the painful aspects of life. It enables us to distance ourselves from our troubles and to see them from a different angle, thereby reducing the pain. That humour performs a vital function of releasing tension has been demonstrated by numerous studies and experiments in the psycho-social field.

A kind of humour which stands midway between laughing with people and irony (that is, laughing *at* others) is the joke or the witticism, analyzed by Freud in a celebrated essay. The key processes involved in the joke are those that find their maximum expression in the comic: condensation, or the union of two previously distinct fields of meaning; inversion, typical of the double entendre; and the shift of a word or phrase from its habitual semantic field to one inappropriate to it. All these processes intervene in our mental habits and disturb our conventional patterns of language and thought to provoke laughter.

If humour has us laughing good-naturedly and unconcernedly at life's troubles, irony is laughter explicitly directed at others, albeit in mild form (irony can be self-irony too when we laugh at that particular 'other' represented by our very self). We most directly laugh at others by means of satire, where the aggressive element is obvious. Satire is a socially acceptable form of aggression, but it imposes the implicit rule that we must be on the side of the satirist, even when it is we who are being lampooned. Satire plays on this complicity or acceptance by its victim, because those who fail to see the joke show themselves to be weak, stupid, or lacking in humour.

Comedy is undoubtedly the most highly developed form of laughter, and it often includes all the others. The comic allows us both to laugh with and to laugh at others, building a bridge between the two dimensions. The essential features of comedy have also been analyzed – in studies of the great comedians, for example – on the basis of a comparison between normal behavior and observed behaviour. We laugh, that is, at the contrast between our normal behaviour and that displayed by the comic. Comedy therefore comprises an element of display; it requires an audience. Whereas irony and the witticism normally involve a three-way interaction between us, the victim and the observer, comedy is addressed to an audience. The classic devices of the comic are exaggeration, inversion, and repetition; and what we laugh at in the comedian's performance is precisely the contrast we draw between us and him: we are never as stupid or accident-prone as the clown or that part of ourselves which provokes our laughter. Thus, the comic gives his spectators a feeling of comparative superiority; the encounter leaves the audience feeling comforted, even victorious. And this brings us back to the theme of danger averted or avoided I introduced in connection with our discussion of phylogenesis. We laugh because, once again, we managed to come out.

Freud explained laughter in these terms, as a form of conservation of energy. Humor and comedy are pleasurable because they enable us to economize on repression. The energy we invest in keeping our unconscious under control is saved, and laughter gives us a kind of covert and instantaneous access to the unconscious, without our having to pass through the sentinel of censorship. Laughter saves what we would have otherwise invested in inhibition, in suffering for life's troubles or in our painful confrontations with others, and hence provokes a sense of relief. Psychoanalytic theory emphasizes another aspect: that laughing involves an act of rebellion by the ego. Through laughter, the ego launches a momentary mutiny against the superego, its grey and severe mentor, and thus releases its aggressiveness in a controlled manner. This controlled liberation of aggressiveness is undoubtedly one component of laughter with a phylogenetic basis, and it is made manifest in irony. One of the essential rules of laughing at others is that the ironist must declare (at least implicitly) that her/his aim is to amuse; that is, s/he makes a *de facto* prior announcement that the aggression is not to be taken as a threat. Agreement is reached with the interlocutor that the irony is intended for the sake of laughter; an agreement which is signalled metalinguistically by the use of such expressions as 'No offence intended'. Alternatively, we attack authority through a third party using irony or satire aimed at a proxy figure. An example of this is provided by the Italian jokes which denigrate the *cara-*

binieri as symbolizing all personal and social authority. Thus when we laugh at the deprived and weak we are in fact laughing, through them, at the great and the powerful.

Cognitive theory has helped to integrate a wholly energy-based, and therefore merely economic, account of laughter (the contribution and the limit of psychoanalysis) with one that explains its properly creative dimension. Laughter thus conceived involves a sudden restructuring of our cognitive field, which associates previously unrelated elements. The juxtaposition of otherwise distant semantic fields creates an unexpected incongruity which is subsequently resolved by laughter. Our hilarity stems from the startling association of heterogeneous materials: we lose our bearings and are momentarily bewildered. Then, equally rapidly, we reconstitute our cognitive patterns by treating the absurd link as comic; what initially struck us as incongruous is assimilated, again discharging the tension.

The cognitive process has, however, its counterpart at the physiological and emotional level, which accounts for the unique quality of this experience. The preliminary phase which prepares us for laughter is marked by an intense mobilization of the emotions, as if we were faced by danger, aggression or the sudden loss of our customary reference points. Then, however, we realize the absence of threat, with a sense of joyful amazement and security taking over, and we allow ourselves the emotional release, the pleasure, of laughter. The instant experience of joy without a proper 'reason' is the emotional core of laughter, which makes it an intensively human experience of gratuitousness.

Laughing and weeping

We laugh, then, about many things; but our laughter also takes many forms. There is the ingratiating laughter with the fixed grimace that we sometimes affect in our dealings with others, especially those more powerful than ourselves. Then there is the defensive laugh, that dry and nervous giggle with which we try to keep unpleasantness at bay, to exorcise the perceived threat in a change of situation or in a difficult encounter. On the other hand, there is the exaggerated guffaw, disproportionate to the content of what we are saying, as if to compensate for some shortcoming or intended to defend ourselves against some implicit accusation. Another variant is the ironic sneer, first directed at ourselves and then generalized as an attack on others and on the world. All these varieties of laughter contained in our everyday social repertoire are entirely distinct from weeping. Weeping is socially perceived as being the reverse of laughter and arises when we confront our suffering in moments of depression, when we wrap ourselves and our lives in a dark shroud.

Our daily laughter is most often 'laughing at', and it is ourselves in fact who are its principal object – at least of the varieties of laughter in the social repertoire that I have just described. Things change when we look at ourselves from a different perspective and create the space that enables us to 'laugh with'. When we renounce the placatory, defensive, or ironic laugh, we begin to 'laugh with'. The distance between laughing and weeping narrows, and we may begin to pass from one to the other more frequently. The change comes about as a different point of view on ourselves and on reality, one which replaces rigidity with fluidity, univocality with plurality, and teaches us that the same thing is not always the same, or not only the same. Unusual juxtapositions become possible, so that what was previously a problem is now seen from a different angle, that the insurmountable difficulty turns out to be different from what we expected. This change of perspective makes room for surprise, moderating any feeling of aggression towards ourselves and others and leaving us instead with *sym-pathy* in the proper sense: the ability to literally 'co-vibrate' with ourselves, others, and things. Irony then, can become a positive process and weds itself with benevolence, an ability to tolerate our own weaknesses and those of others. Or we learn to use it to establish our boundaries, to defend them when they come under attack from others, to settle our scores straightforwardly without resorting to more indirect and covert means.

Our laughter thus becomes a truly free play, and we 'laugh with' ourselves and with others. Laughter and weeping at this point are located on the same emotional continuum. The one may merge with the other because they are the two aspects of the same experience, a contact with reality in which pleasure and pain are present at once. They are human dimensions of experience which are inseparate. Occasional laughter may then be transformed into good humour, a cheerful attitude to life which coexists with pain. The relationship between laughter and weeping grants access to a space of gratuitousness and play, to the element of childishness inherent in all of us.

Good humour is the most stable and the most permanent feature of laughter in that it lives with the possibility of pain and may yield to suffering. Good humour is a state of mind which momentarily emerges or explodes in laughter. Laughter is effectively the simplest and most direct encounter with possibility and the limit; it is the capacity to confront life's troubles with a health-giving medicine which does not deny those troubles and constantly reminds us of them.

The play of the clown

We need this capacity in order to learn how to see what lies before our eyes but goes unnoticed. Our self may learn to play if we allow ourselves to create, to go beyond the limit and open up to the possible still without losing our boundaries. There is an art form, that of the clown, which we may use as a metaphor here. The clown is a double, both White and Black, Good and Evil, Limit and Possibility. Between these two sets of constants the play of 'laughing with' and 'laughing at' unfolds.

The play of the clown contains the flexibility and the reversibility of time, but also a deep awareness of unity. It combines the austerity of ritual with the fancifulness of the game. The art of the clown emerges from a very severe training and a strict respect of the timing of gestures, movements and words: its levity and discontinuity are always the result of a disciplined coordination and a deep interiorization of the rules. A delay of a second in timing, a gesture slightly broader or narrower than what is requested by the situation can transform the potential for laugh into a depressive experience for the audience. The art of the clown invites us to rediscover the pleasure of the play, of a time which can be reversible but does not threaten our inner unity and does never entirely escape the constraint of social rules: the discontinuous sequence of gestures and words that reverses 'real' time and makes us laugh is always supported by an underlying rule to which the clown is committed.

The clown can also teach us a different relation to space. Today, space has become for us an artificial construct which makes it increasingly difficult to maintain the relationship between the mental construct and the physical dimensions in which we nevertheless still move. Both concrete and magical, the space of the clown instead combines the physicality of the motions, bodily exertion, and visibility with the magic of her/his art which expands or breaks down the confines. The clown invites us to learn how to move in different spaces: those of our physical world, increasingly narrow but reminding us of the constraining rules of distance and proximity, dimensions and shapes; and those of virtual realities created by information, where we can open up to our desires and dreams, but where we may also get lost in an erratic wandering. The clown accomplishes his magic task by inducing us to overcome through the imagination the boundaries of the 'real' space, while at the same time he relies on his capacity, carefully trained, to move his body in the physical space and to respect accurately spatial boundaries and constraints.

The art of the clown speaks also of relationships. Today the relation with the other confronts us with choice and with difference. However, the show business society in which we live has taught us a way of looking that simply mirrors what we see and never puts us to the test of difference and of communication. The flat representation of reality provided by the media images substitutes reality itself, depriving us of the possibility to be questioned by difference, to be surprised or threatened by otherness. The clown, as a representative of exaggerated and manifest diversity, forces us into confrontation but still reminds us through his capacity of making us laugh that communication is always possible provided we want it: even the most extreme diversity can be met and become a source of human mutual and pleasant understanding. When we laugh at the mimic and the moves of the clown, so evidently 'other' compared to normal life, we recognize our human features altogether: difference and communication can coexist.

Finally, the art of the clown speaks of wonder. There is no longer room in our culture for mystery, although we still feel the need for contact with the unsayable, with those areas of experience that fall outside calculation and prediction. The enormous spectacle of the media banishes wonder. Everything is designed to tranquillize us; even the most complex matters are dissected and explained. The clown takes us by surprise: he is never what he appears to be, and he helps us to glimpse the mystery that lies in even the simplest things.

When we learn to see what, previously unnoticed, lies before our eyes, we discover that we can weep and laugh. There is the 'head laugh' and the 'belly laugh'. In our culture it is the former that predominates: laughter prompted by mental associations, above all between words and not between bodies, by the speed of images, nods, and winks; a dry, nervous laugh. Laughter which reveals nothing, but which, like the canned laughter of television, connects together the signs of a known universe. The clown's is a belly laugh which stems from our innermost moods; a carnal laugh which provokes sweat and tears. It is a laughter which jolts certainty and brings us momentarily into contact with the unsayable. It establishes an instantaneous relationship between mankind's roots, earth and body, and our need to go beyond the visible façade of things.

It is in this way that our creative resources, so little used, may find expression. The need to go beyond what is present, to discover the hidden face of the moon, seems to lie at the core of many contemporary social practices. It is not by chance that our culture discovers creativity as one of the most central themes, in education and business, in science and organizational life.

Creativity

The theme of creativity is a fashionable one, but the fact itself does not lessen its importance. Why does it command so much of our attention? In the face of rapid and continuous change, the need to develop creative capacities is more urgent than in static and closed systems. The more volatile and open the situation and the more we are required to change by a mutable environment, the more creative qualities become necessary. Flexibility, adaptability, and a capacity for finding new answers for old problems form vital requirements if we are to cope with the constant flux of events. The very differentiation of the processes of accelerated change breaks reality down into ever smaller facets, nullifies solutions adopted in previous contexts, and demands creative responses of us in every situation.

On the other hand, the increasing cerebralization of *homo sapiens* through the development of the neocortex has accentuated inventive and creative capacities of our species over its reproductive function. In the evolution of our species the urge to break with natural constraints and to develop a self-reflexive and symbolic capacity has extended mankind's creative potential. We can interpret the present interest in creativity as signalling a profound change in our evolution, even if the process of 'cerebralization' is still far from advanced and equally distributed, given that much of the population is still wholly excluded from creative resources and forced into repetition, conformism, and standardized consumption.

Creativity is therefore a cultural object which focuses scientific analysis and research, social and organizational practices (as witness the recent boom of creative techniques in management training), and lastly widespread individual needs. The problem of defining the concept of creativity itself testifies to the diversification of the field. We can investigate the origins of the creative capacity and concentrate on the ways in which it develops. We can consider its morphological aspect – that is, the structure of the creative experience – and attribute it to certain qualities of the mind. Or we can examine creativity from the point of view of process and of skills, that is, of creative operations. In this variety of approaches, however, two significant features emerge. Creativity is, first, an activity of the mind which brings cognitive processes and deep-lying affective forces into play. Psychoanalytical theory has suggested that the urge to create the new is rooted in primary experience and expresses the need to protect ourselves against the feeling of guilt over the lost object of our love. More recent cognitive research has stressed the abilities of the mind (such as fluidity, flexibility, originality) and tends to associate creativity with problem-solving. The creative process undoubtedly combines conscious imaginative activity with a more indefinite intuitive sensitivity into which our most intimate affective energies are channelled.

Secondly, the predominant view of creativity today regards it as less closely tied to the extraordinary dimensions of experience and the possession of exceptional qualities. The stereotype of the artist or the inventor has been left behind, and creativity is taken to be one of our various everyday potentials that conscious intervention (personal growth, education, social relations and environment) can stimulate and develop.

These tendencies confirm that the very definition of creativity is becoming a matter of societal debates: a new cultural field is emerging, concerned with the question of how to use and direct our potential. It is becoming more and more obvious that what is required today is not so much problem-solving, where the answer is already implicit in the problem, as the application of our creative capacities to formulating new questions. Identifying creativity with problem-solving we will overlook the fact that creative activity does not necessarily lead to the solution of a given problem, but that it, instead, always requires a restructuring of the field at the level of interrogation. There are creative activities, like art, which do not resolve problems, and there are solutions to problems which are not creative because they are constrained. Our society is confronted with the challenge of encouraging the development of personal resources which enhance the creative process: the acceptance of risk, of the indeterminable, of suspension instead of what is already known, classified, decided; the ability to overcome our inhibitions and our uncertainty concerning ourselves in order to open our minds and to broaden our horizons. Creativity, however we may define it, relies thus on our ability to wonder.

En route ...

The disenchanted heirs of modernity can become Nature only through culture; they can find their natural roots only as a cultural project, through their ability to create and to metacommunicate. Laughter and wonder relate to ethics because they teach us the limit and the possibility of our action, they give us the courage to accept change, and they show us the measure of respect.

We have lost the language of wonder. Pure astonishment requires open eyes and an empty mind – attributes which are rare among the adepts of the technological faith. We are the children of a culture which is still industrial, but which has lost the passion for utopia. The great mainspring of progress no longer drives the clock of history, and we are left the orphans of hope. We are haunted by the past, still desirous about the future but bereft of the comfort of belief. Disenchantment comes to resemble the *terrains vagues* that surround the outer suburbs of our great cities: arid deserts cluttered with the remains of our civilization.

Wonder needs space if it is to take root. We can invest our energies in making room for that which still has no name, work on the path and not just on its end, begin again the rhythmic passage from fullness to emptiness, from movement to standstill. In a disenchanted world which has learned the vanity of the gods and the secular root of things, play and wonder have been banished. Yet we cannot live without them, for our lives are still shrouded with mystery. Creating room for wonderment means that we need to reestablish an innocent relationship with those who are the witnesses to the possible and the unknown: we can start looking at children, other species, traditional cultures, as those who remind us that not everything has been revealed, not everything has been said and, for sure, not everything needs to be said.

Epilogue

Information has today become a central resource and contemporary societies depend on it for their survival and development. The capability of collecting, processing, and transferring information has been developed in the last thirty years to a level which for that period alone goes beyond comparison with all the achievements of the previous history of mankind. As a consequence, the artificial, 'built' character of social life has increased. A large part of our everyday experiences occur in an environment which is entirely produced by society. The media represent and reflect our actions; individuals incorporate and reproduce these messages in a sort of self-propelling spiral. Where are 'nature' and 'reality' outside the cultural representations and images we receive from and produce for our social world? The latter acquires altogether a planetary dimension, and the events are no longer important in themselves or not only for the place and the people where they occur, but for their symbolic impact on the world system.

Information societies develop a cultural production not directly connected to the needs for survival or for reproduction: in that they are 'post-material' societies and they produce a 'cultural surplus'. Control over production, accumulation, and circulation of information depends on codes which organize information and make it understandable. In complex societies, power consists more and more of operational codes, formal rules, knowledge organizers. In its operational logic, information is not a shared resource accessible to everybody, but merely an empty sign, the key to which is controlled by few people only. Access to meaning becomes the field of a new kind of power and conflict.

Social conflicts move to the cultural sphere. They focus on personal identity, the time and space of life, the motivation and codes of daily behaviour. Conflicts lay bare the logic now gaining sway over highly differentiated societies. Complex systems allocate increasing amounts of resources to individuals, who use them to become autonomous loci of action in these systems as effective terminals for processing high-density information. But the systems also exact increasing integration: in order to maintain themselves, they must extend their control through regulation of the deep-seated sources of action and by interfering with the construction of its meaning. Contemporary conflicts bring to the fore actors and forms of action which cannot be fitted into the conventional categories of economic conflict or political competition among interest groups. What lies at the core of contemporary conflicts is the production and reappropriation of meaning.

Over history, societies have progressed through the entire gamut of the resources that drive every living system (matter, energy, information). There have been societies mainly structured on material resources, societies which have depended more on energy for their growth (steam and electricity as the engines of industrialization), and now systems which rely for their survival on information, the control of the environment, expansion into space, and the delicate equilibrium which preserves them from total war. Individually and socially produced identity must constantly cope with the uncertainty created by the ceaseless flow of information, by the fact that individuals belong simultaneously to a plurality of systems, by the variety of their spatio-temporal frames of reference. Identity must therefore be forever reestablished and renegotiated. The search for identity is therefore a remedy against the opacity of the social relations, against uncertainty that constantly constrains action. Producing identity means slowing down the flow of information from the system, making it more stable and coherent; contributing, that is, to the stabilization or modernization of the system itself. But it is not only to the requirement of security and continuity that this search for identity responds. It also provides resources for individuation and enables individuals to perceive themselves as individuals distinct from others and, precisely because of this, to discover in the depth of this separateness the capacity to reject the dominant codes and to reveal their questionable power; it, that is, enables individuals to recognize themselves as producers of meaning and thus to challenge the manipulation of meaning by the apparatuses.

Over the last twenty years, theoretical discussion on the crisis of modernity and research on social practices in everyday life has progressively reinforced the idea that individuals are becoming the social core of what we would have called in more traditional terms 'the social structure': an idea that I first addressed twenty years ago when mainstream sociological debates were still deeply concerned with 'collective' and 'structural' conceptual models that could not easily accept the importance of individual and subjective dimensions of social life. Today the debate over the individual, subjectivity, identity has become a common ground for sociological and political discourse, and probably it is easier to address the character of contemporary social transformation in terms of what I call processes of individuation. Social action, economic investments, and forms of domination are increasingly exerted at the individual level; there is, as it were, a transfer of the structure of society to the individual level. Individuals are provided with resources they put to use within constraints that touch upon their individual life. The filter of intermediate structures such as state, party, family, and interest groups is weakening, and individuals are more directly exposed both to social pressures and to the possibilities or opportunities for action. For at the opposite pole, we continue being confronted with the mega-structures and mega-apparatuses of the mass society. The rift between the latter and what, by stressing only its negative terms, is called individualism, is a feature of present society. Looking at the individual and to her/his inner life is thus not just a psychological point of view any more. Today, it is a strong sociological standpoint that focuses one's attention on individual life as a crucial level of the functioning of present society. With it, a new problem is opened up: how to reestablish or reconstruct the intermediate levels between an individualized/atomized social structure and powerful, anonymous, distant institutions.

There is, however, more than a negative side to individualism. I believe that we are currently witnessing a change in the structure of society that makes individuals central social actors, providing them with resources, capacities, and autonomy as well. This allows them to act as social actors who can be more autonomous, more self-reflective, more responsible, more resourceful; and yet actors who simultaneously become more exposed to social pressures and manipulation which increasingly intervene in the inner structure of individual identity, in the moral, psychological, motivational components of the self. What is taking place before our eyes is thus a social process, not merely a psychological one, and it seems that individualistic reductionism that still characterizes psychology misses this important shift. Today one can no longer address individual issues without a concern for the increasing social intervention in the life of the individual.

This fact also helps to clarify the point of departure in my own work on social movements – they are today more and more obviously located at precisely this border area between the individual and the apparatuses of the system. This is the framework and the source of my questions and theoretical approach to contemporary collective action; social movements are the area in society and everyday social life where these problems are immediately experienced. Movements touch upon the most sensible mechanisms of the society and they come to coincide with the frontiers of change; both as expressions of the 'forces of resistance ('reactionary' and conservative forms of opposing change) and in the form of innovation (creative social initiatives) the issues raised by social movements are always crucial for a given society as a whole. They are in effect indicators of what is taking place in a given society, and today they reveal in many ways the core processes of national societies and our global system alike.

Individuation processes in our time are thus not simply psychological processes but 'structural' tendencies of complex systems. These processes of constructing individual identities, of providing individuals with resources for individuation, ensue from state activities, the education policies, the communication policies. The latter are in fact the many 'public' and 'structural' channels through which individuals are provided with resources for becoming individuals: they are pushed to become individuals and they are also asked to function efficiently as individual agents, as they are expected to develop the capability to process information and properly respond to the information flow.

Contemporary society provides means and resources for individual identification, because there is a space where individuals can become and think of themselves as individuals. Such a space is socially constructed, can be provided because there are resources available. We speak of postmaterial societies, meaning that people have at least solved the basic material needs. Thus there is now a space for thinking of oneself as an individual, and this has been made socially available because of 'structural' reasons. In other societies the idea of oneself as an individual actor was impossible; this, however, does not mean that no individual dimension existed, only that people could identify themselves not as individual actors as such but rather as part of a larger body, a family, a kingdom, state, party, class. No one can claim that all these forms of identification have disappeared; the point is that today far broader spaces have become available for individual identification. Yet this same fact has also become the basis for new forms of inequality as these resources for identification remain unequally distributed: these new forms of structural inequalities are added to the more traditional ones, and at this new level one is 'poor' or 'exploited' when one is deprived of the same right to be an individual. Such a right is distributed unequally and producing great imbalances.

It seems evident that there are, at the macrolevel, tendencies that provide individuals with the possibility of searching for and constructing in full one's own identity. The paradox of the Third World today is that people still need even basic food, while they are simultaneously exposed to the same imaginary world of central societies. The true exploitation does not consist of being deprived of information. People in the *favelas* of Brazil do have information, they can watch television twenty-four hours a day – but they do not have any power to organize this information according to their own needs and their own capacity to respond to those needs. How can we define these new inequalities? If we address them just in terms of traditional deprivation, we will miss a central point. We need an entirely new framework to understand these discriminations and imbalances because in reality the dominant patterns give form to the whole of the system, so that all the previous layers of traditional societies are still there, they will not disappear, but they receive their 'form' from the dominant pattern.

The central role of individual dimension in complex societies in my perspective is neither an individualistic point of view nor simply a 'psychological' dimension. Here it is particularly important to make distinctions, for we are not talking of reality but, instead, we are always engaging different points of view, different levels of analysis. First of all, the individuals we are talking about are part of information systems which make out of them the critical nodes of the production and circulation of a vital social resource, information. Secondly, these individuals remain located within modern states and modern political systems which are more or less democratic, implying more or less participation into the decision-making processes, more or less institutionalized guarantees of individual rights and different procedural systems for participating in such processes. A democratic or an authoritarian regime directly affects our consideration of the status of the individual within a given society. Third, one always has to make an analytical decision and establish the level where to start working on the problem. If we take the example of the genetic engineering, as an extreme issue which is directly linked to the building of individual identities, one can consider it at the level of individual choices and decisions: for instance, couples who cannot have children have expectations towards the scientific advancement of this field so as to be able to fulfil their desire or diminish their fear. One can consider this same issue at the level of public policies, to examine, for instance, whether public policies provide individuals with opportunities for choice or rather impose criteria and rules on individual choice. One can, finally, address the problem at the cultural level and see what kind of values or discourses are born about the issues of genetic intervention on human nature and precisely what are the poles of this new cultural conflict deeply involving individual experience. According to the level chosen for the analysis, we will learn about different aspects of both individual experience and societal problems.

The construction of individual identity is then a risky undertaking. The borderline between pathology and normality is socially established and constructed, it can change and it undergoes shifts that depend on forms of power, types of social relations, and so forth. In our society, there are areas that are frankly and openly defined as pathological, areas of 'normal' behaviour, and in the middle a lot of overlapping situations that are not clearly defined and should be considered by sociologists as very interesting indicators of emerging social trends. The available data shows an increasing presence of 'new' pathologies and psychological troubles. Teenager suicide is a very significant sociological symptom: at a critical passage where identity has to be defined and recognized, and in a certain way closed by establishing the boundaries of an individual self, at this very critical point the possibility of making the closure becomes more and more difficult. In the past, the society itself provided defined channels for making this closure and producing the boundaries that provided the means of delimitation of personal identity. Today's highly differentiated and variable systems are unable to allow the maintenance of the traditional boundaries, while new ways of facilitating the passage are not yet available; it is the young people who suffer from being caught in this uneasy condition more immediately and intimately than others.

A similar observation can be made regarding other passages in life. For the elderly, the prolongation of life faces fewer and fewer technical obstacles, and old people are expected to have a longer, more active life than in the past. But at the same time, the rhetoric of a free and joyful old age to which people are exposed makes very often its mark on the critical social conditions of the majority of the aging part of the population. A complete lack of social markers for the fundamental passage to the old age in life, which is a redefinition of the boundaries in terms of physical possibilities and expectations toward other people, increases the likelihood of new pathologies: those which are not only the traditional mental pathologies of old people but represent new forms of psychological suffering, related to the new paradoxical condition in which it becomes difficult to make sense of the changes implied by aging.

Other forms of psychological suffering arise from the sense of loss fuelled by an excess of symbolic possibilities. The exposure to an unlimited range of symbolic possibilities (goods, relationships, information) creates a clash between the imagined world and the actual access to these chances. People's actual experience, besides being limited by class, gender, race, and age boundaries, remains inevitably below the expectations and dreams fed by the overwhelming exposure to symbolic stimuli. Consequently, frustration and loss are experienced very widely and frequently, feeding new psychological troubles.

We are witnessing a denaturalization of nature and culturalization of conflicts. We are moving from the idea that there is a nature and a body out there, as natural sources of physical and biological events, to the awareness that nature and the body are entirely defined within culture. Paradoxically, today there is no nature left: because of our unprecedented capacity to intervene in nature, the nature we are dealing with, both internally and externally, is the nature we decide to either respect and maintain or change. The Amazonian rain forests and our genes are either respected in their 'natural' state or they are rendered into an arena for manipulation: in both cases they become a field for social intervention, and nature as such will not be preserved unless we decide to keep something outside of our intervention, which is of course a cultural and political decision. Even what we could have called the 'natural' field of social action becomes entirely social and entirely cultural, because it is within this field that nature will be saved, maintained, or violated.

The consequence is that conflicts will increasingly affect the definition of the same field: not just what to do with it but how to name it. Once there is no nature outside the domain of social action intervening deeply in it, the problem will be the agreement or disagreement on the definition of what 'nature' is: and this is not just a matter of words, but implies thorough-going 'material' consequences in technology, economy, organizational power. Nonetheless, the conflict is played out at the level of definition, because the 'experts' increasingly proclaim to us what 'nature' is in a given field (biogenetics, sexuality, environmental issues) and the people affected by this intervention will refuse to understand nature the way those experts want to define it. The field of foreseeable conflicts will then be increasingly within culture, and not between society and something conceived as an external, supposedly pure nature.

Cultural debates and social struggles of this kind will probably bring more clearly to the surface the synchronic dimension of conflicts and the fact that conflicts are played out within the same field, which belongs to both sides and is divided between different definitions. These contrasting definitions struggle for the control of the whole field. For if we, for example, define nature in a certain way, there will be a lot of consequences in terms of technology, economics, politics; if we define it in a different way, the consequences will be completely different. We are already facing these types of debates: think of AIDS, human reproduction or the genetic issues, where the knowledge is always incomplete and often unclear, but entails according to the definition produced by institutional apparatuses significant practical consequences on the policies, the allocation of economic resources, and other arrangements affecting the common life.

Discourses and practices related to the ends of social life are inherently conflictual: there are always two sides on the same issue. The social discourse on the body exemplifies this profound ambivalence. Beginning in the 1960s, the issues of the liberation of the body or the emancipation of sexuality have been raised within a discourse which was partly contradictory with the dominant framework of Western culture, intellectual not physical, rational not emotional. The discourse on the body is, then, simultaneously a continuation of and a challenge to the rationalization processes going on in the West. What is important in this respect is not the discourse itself, but the diffusion of practices concerning the body (from alternative medicine to body awareness, from fitness to meditation and martial arts) that have changed people's everyday lives. In none of these practices the body is entirely reduced to discourse. Culture shifts its attention to the body, but it can never entirely frame the body and render it into a mere message or a symbol: there is always a part of bodily experience which is not translated into language. Feelings, emotions, sensations, and movements are not entirely communicable to others because they also represent the deepest and most intimate parts of human experience.

Culture brings the body to the fore by exalting, on the one hand, its potential as a vehicle for an autonomous individual expression and, on the other, by making out of it the best marketable good. The slow shift towards a bodilization of our culture is neither a process of 'liberation' nor just a new form of rationalization and of hidden manipulation. It contains the seeds of a deep contradiction, for bodily experience inalienably belongs to the individual and only individuals can 'practice' the body. Once the process of an experiential approach to the body is triggered through new forms of awareness, it can never be entirely controlled again. If culture allows people to consciously experience their body, there emerges at least a part of what is lived by individuals which escapes the social discourse, is not included in it, and cannot be entirely controlled. There develops therefore a contradictory potential for change which has been introduced through the diffusion of body practices. Alternative medicines, for example, have rapidly fuelled a new market of professionals, institutions, and health products, but the very fact that through these practices people have an opportunity to experience a different relationship to their body keeps the construction of meaning at least partly open and prevents a complete commodification and manipulation of the body.

We can imagine a society where the capacity for manipulating the body will increase: a deeper penetration into the structure of our genes and into the chemistry of emotions is not just science fiction but a real possibility of the foreseeable future. Yet, unless we think of a system of total domination, there always remains a part of our bodily experience which cannot be entirely culturalized, which belongs to individuals and can become a nucleus of resistance or opposition against external manipulation. This rootedness of human experience in the body provides a potential for change in overculturalized social systems. This is why the action of many recent movements has centred on body awareness and body practices (women's movement, youth movements, movements related to sexuality and health issues). Such forms of collective action have created a broad field of experimentation in body practices which goes far beyond the discourses on the body and which, because of its experiential nature, contributes to the ambivalence I have tried to point out throughout this book.

In complex systems, we are facing an overmentalization of human faculties, even a transferring of human capacities in machines which will contribute to a further expansion of the cortical power of the human species. This overcerebralization of the collective brain, now increasingly embedded in our technology, undermines all the other human capacities related to our feelings, emotions, movement, biological rhythms. The other human 'brains' which connect our species to the evolution of life on Earth ('brains' which govern our biological and sensory experience) are simply denied or ignored. But these seemingly archaic levels of experience, which link us to the chain of biological evolution but are also part of human culture, return and surface in different forms, in illness, everyday ailments, weakening of immune systems, and the like. Instead of being simply denied, these symptomatic signals can be heard and interpreted, and they can be incorporated as part of human experience. In individual practices, bodily experience can contribute to a different cultural direction of complex society. The body can be either 'normalized' through external intervention (medication, intervention on brain chemistry, manipulation of biological rhythms) or become the field for an autonomous and meaningful experience of the many potentials of human species, far beyond its cortical power. This different attitude towards the body is not just an individual choice which can change the direction of everyday life; more than that, it can be the deep texture of broader cultural changes.

It is thus impossible to imagine forms of resistance or opposition to the contemporary manifestations of power which do not involve individual experience. I, however, do not think that it is possible to postulate a kind of an 'uncontaminated' natural core or essence which would withstand and oppose the oversocialized power of manipulation. We only exist within culture and within society, but since we still, and at the same time, belong to nature and carry within ourselves an inner nature the problem is where to draw the borderline. This is a cultural problem, no longer something involving a 'fact' of nature. Even the level at which we decide to halt the destruction of the Amazonian rain forest or stop the intervention by biogenetic engineering will be a fundamentally cultural, political, and social decision. There is nothing preestablished, nothing a priori; there are only the decisions as to where to put the limit, knowing that it in every case must be drawn somewhere because we are not entirely cultural beings, we always remain partly natural beings, we live in an environment, in an ecosystem, and we are a nature in ourselves. But where biology and nature end and culture begins is not decided outside culture. This is the new paradox. We are thus overcultural beings facing the necessity to decide on our own nature. This, again, creates an enormous issue of responsibility with which human beings have never had to cope before.

A power which 'informs' (gives form to) individual life works at the formation of experiential patterns (ideas, images, symbols and emotions). For the very same reason, its interventions are deeply ambivalent. They are less under control than other, more direct and repressive forms of power, those based for example on physical constraints. Acting through codes, messages, and symbols, the new forms of domination are not entirely in control of the effects that they produce. The people's capacity for re-elaboration and reconstruction, a sort of postmodern use of bits of information, of messages, of practices, can produce wholly new and unexpected results; the nature of the resources on which power has to draw remains more ambivalent than that of others in the past. Not all the effects that were aimed for are produced, and there are countereffects.

These issues have been brought to the surface not only in individual practices but by collective actors as well. If the nature of the problems is dilemmatic, we are likely to face forms of collective action that act as interpreters of both poles of these dilemmas. The movements and countermovements serve as the expression of the new struggles for the control of a shared cultural field. Countermovements are often associated with support to the dominant forms of power, but yet they are that never in a linear and transparent way. Even power reflects the dilemmatic nature of the field and is not entirely unified and monolithic. There are divergent orientations among social groups, but there are also contradictions within the elites: the social field in complex societies is multifaceted and cannot be easily unified. We will need therefore an increasingly articulated scheme of interpretation of social movements, for there are never just two poles in a conflict, but, instead, many different forms of its expression. Countermovements, in fact, can tell us a lot about the nature of the field and they serve as signals of what a conflict is about.

Being strictly related to individual experience in everyday life, these forms of collective action are apparently very weak and certainly they do not seem to much affect the structure of society and its political decision-making. But their apparent weakness is in fact the most appropriate way to oppose a power that has become molecular and penetrates individual lives: even the preconditions for individual action are at stake – the structure of the brain, the relational patterns, the biology of emotions.

In order to keep this ambivalence open, there is, of course a second step to be completed: the political conditions which create the space for this pluralist game of meaning. Having stressed the central importance of the cultural dimension, at the end we come back to the importance of politics. Only if some conditions of open manifestation of this ambivalence are guaranteed it can be transformed into creative action. This is the new problem of democracy: What are the political conditions that allow these seeds of ambivalence and plurality of meaning to develop in new forms of action? How can collective action emerge and bring the issues to the political systems as agendas for decision making, as creation of new rules, as new guarantees of rights for individual and group experience in everyday life?

We have to expect movements and countermovements because the issue that is raised is always a dilemmatic one. The problem with a system that has reached its limits, that has no space or time left outside of it, is that the issues have become entirely internal. There is not a future society waiting for us which will substitute the present one and give a final solution to its contradictions. We can only think of different ways to manage our dilemmas. The example of the relationship to nature, whether internal or external, is one of the most significant: we cannot choose between nature and technology, we can only manage different blends of technological intervention and respect for nature. There is no possibility of escaping the necessary link between these two poles. In the same way, we cannot choose between globalization and particularism. The respect for differences and the necessity of reaching a global integration of the world system and making it work cannot be separated. We can only manage different political solutions to cope with these dilemmas. In our lives and in our politics courage and hope will be our companions.

Bibliographical note

In this note I have collected and organized by themes my essential references, whose comprehensive list is provided at the end of the book. This short bibliographical essay is meant to replace notes or references incorporated in the text, with the purpose of easing the reader's task and not burdening him/her with a display of my accumulated knowledge and academic correctness. This note is also designed for readers wishing to explore further the themes discussed in each chapter. The references listed represent only some of the many books which helped me to develop my ideas and they are restricted, with some exceptions, to works published in the last ten years. Chronology in not in itself an equivalent for quality, but the most recent works have generally the advantage of presenting a cumulative and up-to-date synthesis of the previous debates and findings. They can therefore provide useful guidelines for further study.

The general framework of the book refers to the current debates on contemporary society, the present role of culture, the place of individual experience in complex systems, and the implications of societal changes for the theory of social action. My basic phenomenological perspective has been exposed to many influences and many challenges. The texture of the book implies an underlying dialogue with such authors as Alain Touraine (1984, 1994); Jürgen Habermas (1984, 1989, 1987, 1990); Jeffrey Alexander (1988a, 1988b, 1989); Pierre Bourdieu (1984, 1990); Michel Foucault (1970, 1979, 1980); Anthony Giddens (1984, 1990, 1991); Norbert Elias (1991, 1994); Zygmunt Bauman (1991, 1992). Some of the philosophical questions raised by Charles Taylor (1989, 1992b) and Richard Rorty (1989) are also echoed in the text.

My reflection on culture is indebted to Mary Douglas (1970, 1986, 1992) and Clifford Geertz (1973, 1983): for an overview of current debates see also Wutnow (1987) and Alexander and Seidman (1988). The book also assumes that hermeneutics has introduced our time into a new way of hearing, reading and seeing (Ricoeur 1974, 1976, 1984). The cognitive revolution initiated by Jerome Bruner (1986, 1990, 1991) is also acknowledged as a fundamental step towards a new paradigm. The contributions of social psychology in terms of scripts (Schank and

Abelson 1977), social representations (Farr and Moscovici 1984), the rhetorical construction of arguments and thoughts (Billig 1987) are constituent parts of the theoretical background of this book, as well as the reflections on the discoursive construction of identity (Shotter and Gergen 1989; Gergen 1991; Harré and Gillett 1994).

The paradigm that stresses the capacity of human action to construct meaning and making sense of reality has been cross-fertilized by its meeting with environmental concerns: the seminal work of Gregory Bateson (1972, 1979, 1991) has opened a path which has been enriched by the contribution of theorists belonging to different fields: see Maturana and Varela (1980); Watzlawick (1984); Capra (1982); Morin (1980, 1986); Roszak (1992).

The dimension of the everyday has been brought to the surface of social life as a fundamental constituent of experience and the formation of meaning (see Lalive d'Epinay 1983 and de Certeau 1984); the reflection on women's condition and experience has contributed in a decisive way to this understanding (see Chodorow 1979, 1989; Gilligan 1982; Gilligan *et al.* 1988).

Recent debates on modernity and postmodernity are producing an increasing amount of literature, whose main concern is, implicitly or explicitly, to answer the question of what kind of society we are living in. Apart from the already mentioned works by Touraine (1984), Giddens (1990, 1991), Taylor (1989) and Bauman (1991, 1992), the reader can refer to Huyssen (1986) and Jameson (1991). Some significant references presenting a synthesis of the current debate are Harvey (1989), Turner (1990), Rose (1991), Denzin (1991), Lash and Friedman (1992); Seidman and Wagner (1992), Smart (1992). The question concerning the nature of contemporary society is more explicitly addressed by Lash and Urry (1987), Crook *et al.* (1992) and Beck (1992).

The analyses of popular culture and consumer culture, as well as the increasing role of the media are also an important part of the reflection on contemporary society. On popular culture see Chambers (1985, 1986, 1994); Modleski (1986); Fiske (1987, 1989); Hebdige (1988); Willis (1990); Mukerji and Schudson (1991); Morley (1992). On popular music, the reader can refer to Chambers (1985); Frith and Goodwin (1990); Middleton (1990). On the consumer culture some essential references are Tomlison (1990); Shields (1992), Featherstone (1992) and Yannis and Lang (1995). The role of the media in creating a global culture is analyzed by Salmon (1989); Ferguson (1990); McQuail (1992) and Robertson (1992).

Finally, the literature on social movements in contemporary societies provides an important theoretical and empirical contribution to both cultural and political changes that simultaneously involve and affect individual life. For a general theory of collective action in the information age, see Melucci (1996). The relation between movements and institutions is the main focus of Alberoni (1984). For a synthesis of the current debate on social movements, see Morris and McClurg Mueller (1992); Maheu (1995). On the 'novelty' of contemporary movements see Melucci (1989); Mica (1992); Larana *et al.* (1994). The cultural aspects are discussed in depth by Johnston and Klandermans (1995) and Darnowsky *et al.*

(1995). The political impact of social movements is dealt with by Hall and Jacques (1989); Dalton (1990); Tarrow (1994). The perspective of a different relationship between social action, politics and civil society is discussed by Goldfarb (1991) and Arato and Cohen (1992).

Chapter 1

The reader may refer for guidance through the immense literature on representations of time to an overview provided by Adam (1990) and Hassard (1990); and, among the most outstanding books on the subject, to Elias (1993). On time as a psychological experience and on its distortions, see McGrath and Kelly (1986) and McGrath (1988). Measurements of time in the modern age have been studied by a number of historians: see for example Cipolla (1967), Landes (1984) and Aveni (1989). The modern conception of time and its change is also discussed by Luhmann (1987) and Novotny (1992). The reference to the clock as an external measurement of time is to be found in Pessoa (1991).

On memory and experience, see in particular Namer (1987) and on the collective dimensions of memory Halbwachs (1975); Shils (1981); Middleton and Edwards (1990). The pattern of the spiral is the subject of a book by Purce (1974) which contains a wealth of reference to other cultures.

On the construction of space in our culture, the reader is referred to the fundamental work of Henri Lefebvre (1991) and to the essays collected by Gregory and Urry (1985). On the space in urban settings, see Sennett (1993) and on the changes of space toward the virtual dimension, see Benedikt (1991) and Woolley (1992). Norman (1988) has considered the relation with everyday life objects as a spatial and perceptive experience.

A general introduction to the topic of rhythms is provided by Von Franz (1978) and the relation between rhythms and biology is analyzed by Winfree (1987). For a reflection on time rhythms and bodily experience, see Charmaz (1992); on the relation with dreams, see Mindell (1985). The social organization of time has been specially analyzed by Zerubavel (1981, 1985). Gender differences in relation to time have been analyzed by Forman and Sowton (1989); Davies (1989); Shelton (1992). For the organization of work time and its changes, see Sirianni (1988) and more generally Young (1988).

A general overview of the most advanced scientific patterns of time and space, both in theoretical and experiential terms, see Peat (1987); Briggs and Peat (1989); Baker (1993).

Chapter 2

Contemporary discussion on the topic of identity encompasses both the biological and social sciences and has important philosophical repercussions. For an introduction, see Hirsch (1982); Shaver (1985); Abrams and Hogg (1990); Whyte (1992); Suls (1993); and Fitzgerald (1993). For reflection on needs combining biology and culture, the reader is referred to Vincent (1986); Dennett (1988, 1991); and Laughlin *et al.* (1990). An analysis of identity transformations during the life cycle can be found in Levinson (1978); on female identity in particular, Gilligan (1982); and Jardine (1985). The social psychological perspective is particularly rich in providing an understanding of the different facets of the self: see Burkitt (1991); Gergen (1991); Breakwell (1992); Harré and Gillett (1994). For the debate on the continuity and discontinuity of identity, see Parfit (1984); Pizzorno (1993) and Barglow (1994). The breakdown of identity is discussed by Kristeva (1989) and Baumeister (1991). The experience of madness is dealt with in Foucault (1967, 1979); Canguilhem (1989) and Scull (1993), while the psychiatric institution and the relationship between emancipation and control are analysed in Castel (1988); Busfield (1989); and Luske (1990). On the debate over deinstitutionalization, see Elizur and Minuchin (1989); Braden Johnson (1990); and Isaac and Armat (1990).

Chapter 3

The essential references on the multiplication of the self include Elster (1985); Lasch (1984); Gergen (1991); Csikszentmihalyi (1994). Berger *et al.* (1973) first analysed the homelessness of the mind. From a psychological standpoint, research into the plurality of intelligences has reinforced the idea of a multiple self: see Gardner (1983). Analysis of presentness has benefited from innovative contributions by research into optimal experience and the flow of consciousness: for a summary, see Csikszentmihalyi and Csikszentmihalyi (1988); Csikszentmihalyi (1990). The difficulties in maintaining the boundaries and the continuity of the self in terms of depression (Kristeva 1989) or other psychological troubles (Baumeister 1991, Gergen 1991) are often seen as the other face of individualism (Lasch 1980; Dumont 1983; Bellah *et al.* 1985), while this book tries to propose a more nuanced frame to account for the need for individuation in complex systems.

Chapter 4

The importance of a change of perspective when considering the relationship between ecosystem and society has been especially stressed by Capra (1982) and Morin (1980, 1986). For discussion of an ecology of the mind, see Bateson (1972, 1979, 1991). Regarding the vast literature on the brain for a preliminary introduction see Changeux (1985); Oakley (1985); and Humphrey (1992). An overview of developments in the neurosciences is provided by Adelman (1987); Kosslyn and Andersen (1992) and Klivingston (1993). On network models, see Gazzaniga (1987, 1993); Calvin (1989). The split-brain research is summarized in Davidson and Hugdahl (1994). On neurotransmitters see in particular Snyder (1989). The relationship between brain and immune system is discussed in Ornstein and Sobel (1987). The dreaming activity of the brain is one of the most interesting chapters in contemporary research: see Hobson (1988). On the relationship between brain and biological rhythms see Winfree (1987).

Chapter 5

The ambivalence of the body and its role in contemporary culture is treated by Feathersone *et al.* (1991); Shilling (1993); and Falk (1994). The relationship between the body, mental life and the emotions is discussed by Vincent (1986); Johnson (1987) and Murphy (1992). Murphy also widely discusses the body's relationship with pain and its languages, which is also analyzed by Shorten (1992); Levin and Salomon (1990) and Freund (1990). For the communicative dimension of the body, the reader can refer to Turner (1982); O'Neil (1989); and Taussig (1993).

On birth control, see the literature referred to below for chapter 8. Death as a social phenomenon in contemporary system has been widely discussed by Baudrillard (1993). Several important studies have carefully analyzed the social organization of death: see Momeyer (1988); Prior (1989); Nearl (1989); Field (1989). For a recent synthesis of theory and research, see Clark (1993). An approach that links the experience of dying to the postmodern condition and its ethical implications is offered by Bauman (1993a).

Chapter 6

Prevention policies and the therapeutization of everyday life are analysed in Donzelot (1979, 1984). On non-institutional medicines the growing body of research provides a wide spectrum for comparison: see Salmon (1984); Frohoc (1992); and Wardwell (1994). The increasing inclusion of alternative practices into the medical establishment is discussed by Sharma (1993); Gillett (1994) and Wolpe (1994). For discussion of psychotherapy and the importance of the relationship as the basic healing factor, see Fancher (1994). For an analysis of the possibilities and limits of medicine, see Gilman (1988); Turner (1992) and Lupton (1994). Therapy as a social contruction is discussed by McNamee and Gergen (1992).

Gilman also discusses social images of illness from madness to AIDS. For a specific consideration of AIDS as one of most dramatic examples of terminal illnesses, both from the personal and the institutional point of view, see Aggleton *et al.* (1990) and Ornstein (1992). More generally on the relationship between medicine, emergencies and terminal illnesses see Anspach (1993).

Chapter 7

The term culture of narcissism comes from the widely-discussed book by Christopher Lasch (1978). The passionate account of the Guayaki culture is by Pierre Clastres (1977). On the topic of otherness see Fabian (1983) and de Certeau (1986). The symbolic dimension of difference and the relationship between difference and inequality is discussed by Lamont and Fournier (1992). Gayatri Spivak (1987) has also discussed otherness both as cultural difference and inequality.

In the growing body of research on old people a summary is provided by Binstock and Shanas (1985). For recent developments of theory and research, see

Pratt and Norris (1994) and Thorson (1995). On the ages of life, see Levinson (1978). Important references in the immense literature on youth culture are Hall and Jefferson (1979) and Hebdige (1979). For a history of youth as a social condition see Mitterauer (1992). Recent changes in the 'postmodern' youth culture have been discussed by Dubet (1987); Willis (1990); Coupland (1991); and Ziehe (1991). For a recent synthesis of theory and research, see Fornas and Bolin (1995).

On male and female, the reader is referred to the growing literature on gender, where the self-reflective work produced by women on feminine identity is much richer than its counterpart on male's condition and identity. Beyond the classics of feminism some recent references are Haug (1987) on female sexualization; Smith (1988) on women's experience in everyday life; Apter (1990), Bjerrum Nielsen and Rudberg (1994) and Johnson (1993) on the formation of feminine identity, particularly in the relationship between mothers and daughters. Modleski (1982) has discussed the role of mass culture in women's self-representations. For a general discussion of the women's condition after feminism, see Modleski (1991); Butler (1991) and Lorber (1994). Changes in masculine identity are discussed by Bly (1990); Keen (1991); and Badinter (1992). On fatherhood and its changing role, see Hanson and Bozett (1985); Robinson and Barret (1986); and Lamb (1987). On the affective dimension of relationships, see more generally Hinde (1987) and Duck (1993). For the changing role of emotions in social action, see Frijda (1986); Flam (1990a, 1990b).

Culture as difference is becoming a central problem in the issue of multiculturalism. For a general discussion, see in particular Taylor (1992a); Locke (1992); Friedman (1994) and Maffesoli (1995). On nations and nationalism, see Giddens (1985); Anderson (1991); Schlesinger (1991) and Greenfield (1992). On ethnicity, see in particular Gilroy (1987, 1993a, 1993b); Cornell (1988) and Kepel (1987; 1994). For the American debate on political correctedness, see Berman (1992) and Hugues (1993). Ethical implications of a highly differentiated world are discussed by Taylor (1992b) and Bauman (1993b).

Chapter 8

For a discussion on reproductive techniques, see Corea (1985); Field (1988); and Bonnicksen (1989). The relationship between the woman's body and scientific discourse is analyzed by Jacobus *et al.* (1990). The relationship between eros, sexuality and love in the modern world is discussed by Foucault (1980); D'Emilio and Friedman (1988); and Giddens (1992). On love and falling in love, see in particular Alberoni (1983). For the redefining of the paternal and maternal figure, see the references for the previous chapter.

Chapter 9

The analyses by Bateson, Morin, and Capra extend ecological debate beyond problems of pollution. The global dimension of today's world problems implies a redefinition of what is still defined as the 'international' system. The dramatic clivages of this system are analyzed by Adams (1993). The discussion of a different world order is at the core of present debates among the students of international relations. For an overview of the prospects of a new cosmopolis see Toulmin (1990) and on the loss of meaning of the world system Laidi (1994). Richard Falk (1992) is among those who have more directly addressed the issue of a different world order. For the role of grassroot movements in globalizing the issues, see Ekins (1992). On the globalization of politics, the reader can refer to Luard (1990) and McGrew and Lewis (1992). A key role in this process is played by a new global political economy of communication (see Comor 1994). The emerging field of new rights is discussed by Galtung (1994), while the moral status of just and unjust wars as discussed by Walzer (1992 (1977)) has dramatically changed after the Gulf War and the fundamental role played by the media system in it: see Wolton (1991); Smith (1992).

Chapter 10

On laughter in its various dimensions, see Chapman and Foot (1976a, 1976b) and McGhee and Goldstein (1983). Children humor and gender differences in laughing are analyzed by McGhee and Chapman (1980) and Lundell (1993). Humor as a cultural experience is discussed by Porteous (1989); Oring (1992) and Hall *et al.* (1993). On the comic in different cultural contexts, see Siegel (1987) and Stebbins (1990). The connection between laughing and crying as human emotional experiences is analyzed by Plessner (1970) and Grathoff (1970). For the cultural roots of crying and the gender markers of this experience, see Frey and Langseth (1985); Lombardo *et al.* (1983); and Askew and Ross (1988).

Federico Fellini, besides his movies, has condensed in a passionate book his love for the clowns (Fellini 1970). A stimulating analysis of the clown and the circus culture has been provided by Bouissac (1976). For the history of circus and the role of the clown, see Thetard (1978). Jean Starobinski (1983) has proposed a rich theoretical analysis of the relationship between the clown, art and culture. For more recent and very detailed semiotic analysis of the clown performance, see Little (1991, 1993).

Creativity has become over the last twenty years a very attractive cultural topic and an increasing body of literature is devoted to different aspects of creative experience in various contexts. For a general introduction to the theories of creativity, see Sternbeg (1988) and Runco and Albert (1990). For the psychoanalytic and cognitive approaches, see respectively Arieti (1976) and Weisberg (1986). For approaches that stress the cognitive and social dimensions of creativity, see Boden (1990); Joas (1992); Gardner (1993) and White (1993). The role of intrinsic motivation has been pointed out by Deci and Ryan (1985) and developed by Csikszentmihalyi (1990). For creativity in the arts, see Zolberg (1990). The process of scientific discovery and the role of scientific institutions in enhancing or impeding creativity is analyzed by Latour (1987); Root-Bernstein (1989); Binnig (1989); and Margolis (1993). Agor (1989) offers an overview of the role of creative qualities in organizations.

References

Abrams, Dominic and Hogg, Michael A. (eds.) 1990, *Social Identity Theory*, Hemel Hempstead: Harvester.

Adam, Barbara E. 1990, *Time and Social Theory*, Cambridge: Polity Press.

Adams, Nassau A. 1993, *Worlds Apart: The North–South Divide and the International System*, London: Zed Books.

Adelman, George (ed.) 1987, *Encyclopaedia of Neurosciences*, Boston: Birkhauser.

Aggleton, Peter, Davies, Peter and Hart, Graham (eds.) 1990, *AIDS: Individual, Cultural and Policy Dimensions*, London: Falmer Press.

Agor, Weston H. (ed.) 1989, *Intuition in Organizations*, Newbury Park: Sage.

Alberoni, Francesco 1983, *Falling in Love*, New York: Random House.

  1984, *Movement and Institution*, New York: Columbia University Press.

Alexander, Jeffrey C. 1988a, *Action and Its Environment: Towards a New Synthesis*, New York: Columbia University Press.

  1988b, *Durkheimian Sociology: Cultural Studies*, Cambridge: Cambridge University Press.

  1989, *Structure and Meaning: Relinking Classical Sociology*, New York: Columbia University Press.

Alexander, Jeffrey C. and Seidman, Steven (eds.) 1988, *Culture and Society: Contemporary Debates*, Cambridge: Cambridge University Press.

Anderson, Benedict 1991, *Imagined Communities*, London: Verso.

Anspach, Renee R. 1993, *Deciding Who Lives: Fateful Choices in the Intensive-Care Nursery*, Berkeley: University of California Press.

Apter, Terri 1990, *Altered Loves: Mother and Daughters during Adolescence*, New York: St. Martin's Press.

Arato, Andrew and Cohen, Jean 1992, *Civil Society and Social Theory*, Cambridge MA: MIT Press.

Arieti, Silvano 1976, *The Magic Synthesis*, New York: Basic Books.

Askew, Sue and Ross, Carol 1988, *Boys Don't Cry*, Milton Keynes: Open University Press.

Aveni, Anthony F. 1989, *Empires of Time: Calendars, Clocks and Cultures*, New York: Basic Books.

Badinter, Elisabeth 1992, *XY: De l'identité Masculine*, Paris: Odile Jacob.

Baker, Patrick L. 1993, 'Space, Time, Space-Time and Society', *Sociological Inquiry*, 63, 4: 406–24.

Barglow, Raymond 1994, *The Crisis of the Self in the Age of Information: Computers, Dolphins and Dreams*, London: Routledge.

Bateson, Gregory 1972, *Steps to an Ecology of Mind*, New York: Ballantine.

1979, *Mind and Nature*, New York: E. P. Dutton.

1991, *A Sacred Unity: New Steps to an Ecology of Mind*, San Francisco: Harper.

Baudrillard, Jean 1993, *Symbolic Exchange and Death*, London: Sage.

Bauman, Zygmunt 1991, *Modernity and Ambivalence*, Cambridge: Polity Press.

1992, *Intimations of Postmodernity*, London: Routledge.

1993a, *Mortality, Immortality and Other Life Strategies*, Cambridge: Polity Press.

1993b, *Postmodern Ethics*, Oxford: Blackwell.

Baumeister, Roy F. 1991, *Escaping the Self: Alcoholism, Spirituality, Masochism and Other Flights from the Burden of Selfhood*, New York: Basic Books.

Beck, Ulrich 1992, *Risk Society. Towards a New Modernity*, London: Sage.

Bellah, Robert N., Marsden, Richard, Sullivan, William M., Swidler, Ann and Tipton, Steven M. 1985, *Habits of the Heart. Individualism and Commitment in American Life*, Berkeley: University of California Press.

Benedikt, Michael (ed.) 1991, *Cyberspace: First Steps*, Cambridge, MA: MIT Press.

Berger, Peter L., Berger B. and Kellner, H. 1973, *The Homeless Mind*, Harmondsworth: Penguin.

Berman, Paul (ed.) 1992, *Debating P.C.: The Controversy Over Political Corectedness on College Campuses*, New York: Dell

Billig, Michael 1987, *Arguing and Thinking: A Rethorical Approach to Social Psychology*, Cambridge: Cambridge University Press.

Binnig, Gerd 1989, *Aus dem Nichts*, Munich: R.Piper.

Binstock, Robert H. and Shanas, Ethel (eds.) 1985, *Handbook of Aging and the Social Sciences*, New York: Van Nostrand.

Bjerrum Nielsen, Harriet and Rudberg, Monica 1994, *Psychological Gender and Modernity*, Oslo: Scandinavian University Press.

Bly, Robert 1990, *Iron John*, New York: Addison-Wesley.

Boden, Margaret A. 1990, *The Creative Mind*, New York: Basic Books.

Bonnicksen, Andrea L. 1989, *In Vitro Fertilization: Building Policies from Laboratories to Legislatures*, New York: Columbia University Press.

Bouissac, Paul 1976, *Circus and Culture: A Semiotic Approach*, Bloomington IN: Indiana University Press.

Bourdieu, Pierre 1984, *Distinction: A Social Critique of the Judgement of Taste*, London: Routledge.

1990, *In Other Words: Essays Towards a Reflexive Sociology*, Cambridge: Polity Press.

Braden Johnson, Ann 1990, *Out of Bedlam: The Truth about Deinstitutionalization*, New York: Free Press.

Breakwell, Glynis M. (ed.) 1992, *Social Psychology of Identity and the Self Concept*, London: University of Surrey Press.

Briggs, John and Peat, F. David 1989, *Turbulent Mirror: An Illustrated Guide to Chaos Theory and the Science of Wholeness*, New York: Harper and Row.

Bruner, Jerome 1986, *Actual Minds, Possible Worlds*, Cambridge MA: Harvard University Press.

1990, *Acts of Meaning*, Cambridge MA: Harvard University Press.

1991, 'The Narrative Construction of Reality', *Critical Inquiry*, 18: 1–21.

Burkitt, Ian 1991, *Social Selves: Theories of the Social Formation of Personality*, London: Sage.

Busfield, Joan 1989, *Managing Madness: Changing Ideas and Practice*, London: Unwin Hyman.

Butler, Judith 1991, *Gender Trouble*, London: Routledge.

Calvin, William H. 1989, *The Cerebral Symphony*, New York: Bantam Books.

Canguilhem, Georges 1989, *The Normal and the Pathological*, New York: Zone Books.

Capra, Fritjof 1982, *The Turning Point*, New York: Simon and Schuster.

Castel, Robert 1988, *The Regulation of Madness: The Origins of Incarceration in France*, Berkeley: University of California Press.

Chambers, Iain 1985, *Urban Rhythms: Pop Music and Popular Culture*, London: Macmillan.

1986, *Popular Culture: The Metropolitan Experience*, London: Methuen.

1994, *Migrancy, Culture and Identity*, London: Routledge.

Changeux, Paul 1985, *Neuronal Man: The Biology of Mind*, Oxford: Oxford University Press.

Chapman, Anthony J. and Foot, Hugh C. (eds.) 1976a, *Humor and Laughter: Theory, Research and Applications*, Chichester: Wiley.

1976b, *It's a Funny Thing Humor*, Oxford: Pergamon Press.

Charmaz, Kathy 1992, *Good Days, Bad Days: The Self in Chronic Illness and Time*, New Brunswick: Rutgers University Press.

Chodorow, Nancy 1979, *The Reproduction of Mothering*, Berkeley: University of California Press.

1989, *Feminism and Psychoanalytic Theory*, New Haven: Yale University Press.

Cipolla, Carlo M. 1967, *Clocks and Culture 1300-1700*, London: Collins.

Clark, David (ed.) 1993, *The Sociology of Death*, Oxford: Blackwell.

Clastres, Pierre 1977, *Society against the State*, Oxford: Blackwell.

Comor, Edward A. (ed.) 1994, *The Global Political Economy of Communication*, London: Macmillan.

Corea, Gena 1985, *The Mother Machine: Reproductive Technologies from Artificial Insemination to Artificial Wombs*, New York: Harper and Row.

Cornell, Stephen 1988, *The Return of the Native: American Indian Political Resurgence*, Oxford: Oxford University Press.

Coupland, Douglas 1991, *Generation X*, London: Abacus.

Crook, Stephen, Pakulski, Jan and Waters, Malcolm 1992, *Postmodernization: Change in Advanced Society*, London: Sage.

Csikszentmihalyi, Mihaly 1990, *Flow: The Psychology of Optimal Experience*, New York: Harper.

1993, *The Evolving Self*, New York: Harper.

Csikszentmihalyi, Mihaly and Csikszentmihalyi, Selega I. (eds.) 1988, *Optimal Experience*, Cambridge: Cambridge University Press.

D'Emilio, John and Freedman, Estelle B. 1988, *Intimate Matters: A History of Sexuality in America*, New York: Harper and Row.

Dalton, Russell J. and Kuechler, Manfred (eds.) 1990, *Challenging the Political Order: New Social and Political Movements in Western Democracies*, Oxford: Oxford University Press.

Darnowsky, Marcy, Epstein, Barbara and Flacks, Richard (eds.) 1995, *Cultural Politics and Social Movements*, Philadelphia: Temple University Press.

Davidson, Richard and Hugdahl, Kenneth (eds.) 1994, *Brain Asymmetry*, Cambridge MA: MIT Press.

Davies, Karen 1989, *Women and Time*, University of Lund.

De Certeau, Michel 1984, *The Practice of Everyday Life*, Berkeley: University of California Press.

1986, *Heterologies: Discourse on the Other*, Manchester: Manchester University Press.

Deci, Edward L. and Ryan, Richard M. 1985, *Intrinsic Motivation and Self-Determination in Human Behavior*, New York: Plenum.

Dennett, Daniel C. 1988, *The Intentional Stance*, Cambridge MA: MIT Press.

1991, *Consciousness Explained*, Boston: Little, Brown and Co.

Denzin, Norman 1991, *Image of Postmodern Society*, London: Sage.

Donzelot, Jacques 1979, *The Policing of Families*, London: Hutchinson.

1984, *L'Invention du Social*, Paris: Fayard.

Douglas, Mary 1970, *Purity and Danger*, Harmondsworth: Penguin.

1986, *How Institutions Think*, New York: Syracuse University Press.

1992, *Risk and Blame*, London: Routledge.

Dubet, François 1987, *La Galère: Jeunes en Survie*, Paris: Fayard.

Duck, Steven W. (ed.) 1993, *Individuals in Relationships*, London: Sage.

Dumont, Louis 1983, *Essai sur l'Individualisme*, Paris: Seuil.

Ekins, Paul 1992, *A New World Order: Grass Root Movements for Global Change*, London: Routledge.

Elias, Norbert 1991, *The Society of Individuals*, Oxford: Blackwell.

1993, *Time: An Essay*, Oxford: Blackwell.

1994, *The Civilizing Process*, Oxford: Blackwell.

Elizur, Joel and Minuchin, Salvador 1989, *Institutionalizing Madness: Families, Therapy and Society*, New York: Basic Books.

Elster, Jon (ed.) 1985, *The Multiple Self*, Cambridge: Cambridge University Press.

Fabian, Johannes 1983, *Time and the Other: How Anthopology Makes Its Other*, New York: Columbia University Press.

Falk, Pasi 1994, *The Consuming Body*, London: Sage.

Falk, Richard A. 1992, *Exploration at the Edge of Time: The Prospects for World Order*, Philadelphia: Temple University Press.

Fancher, Robert 1994, *Cultures of Healing: Correcting the Image of American Mental Health Care*, New York: W. H. Freeman.

Farr, Robert M. and Moscovici, Serge (eds.) 1984, *Social Representations*, Cambridge: Cambridge University Press.

Featherstone, Mike 1992, *Consumer Culture and Postmodernism*, London: Sage.

Featherstone, Mike, Hepworth, Mike and Turner, Bryan S. (eds.) 1991, *The Body: Social Process and Cultural Theory*, London: Sage.

Fellini, Federico 1970, *I clown*, Bologna: Cappelli.

Ferguson, Marjorie (ed.) 1990, *Public Communication: The New Imperatives*, London: Sage.

Field, David 1989, *Nursing the Dying*, London: Routledge.

Field, Martha A. 1988, *Surrogate Motherhood: The Legal and Human Issues*, Cambridge MA: Harvard University Press.

Fiske, John 1987, *Television Culture*, London: Methuen.

1989, *Understanding Popular Culture*, Boston: Unwin Hyman.

Fitzgerald, Thomas K. 1993, *Metaphors of Identity*, New York: SUNY Press.

Flam, Helena 1990a, 'Emotional Man. I. The Emotional Man and the Problem of Collective Action', *International Sociology*, 5, 1: 39–56.

1990b, 'Emotional Man. II. Corporate Actors as Emotion-Motivated Emotional Managers', *International Sociology*, 5, 2: 225–34.

Forman, Frieda Johles and Sowton, Caoran (eds.) 1989, *Taking Our Time: Feminist Perspectives on Temporality*, Oxford: Pergamon Press.

Fornas, Johan and Bolin, Goran 1995, *Youth Culture in Late Modernity*, London: Sage.

Foucault, Michel 1967, *Madness and Civilization: A History of Insanity in the Age of Reason*, London: Tavistock.

1970, *The Order of Things*, London: Tavistock Publications.

1979, *Discipline and Punish: The Birth of Prison*, New York: Vintage/Random.

1980, *A History of Sexuality*, New York: Vintage.

1980, *Power/Knowledge*, New York: Pantheon.

Freund, Peter E. S. 1990, 'The Expressive Body: A Common Ground for the Sociology of Emotions and Health and Illness', *Sociology of Health and Illness*, 12, 4: 452–77.

Frey, William H. and Langseth, Muriel 1985, *The Mystery of Tears*, Minneapolis: Winston Press.

Friedman, Jonathan 1994, *Cultural Identity and Global Process*, London: Sage.

Frijda, Nico H. 1986, *The Emotions*, Cambridge: Cambridge University Press.

Frith, Simon and Goodwin, Andrew (eds.) 1990, *On Record: Rock, Pop and the Written Word*, New York: Pantheon Books.

Frohoc, Fred M. 1992, *Healing Powers: Alternative Medicine, Spiritual Communities and the State*, Chicago: University of Chicago Press.

Galtung, Johan 1994, *Human Rights in Another Key*, Cambridge: Polity Press.

Gardner, Howard 1983, *Frames of Mind*, New York: Basic Books.

1993, *Creating Minds*, New York: Basic Books.

Gazzaniga, Michael S. 1987, *The Social Brain*, New York: Basic Books.

1993, *Nature's Mind*, New York: Basic Books.

Geertz, Clifford 1973, *The Interpretation of Cultures*, New York: Basic Books.

1983, *Local Knowledge*, New York: Basic Books.

Gergen, Kenneth J. 1991, *The Saturated Self: Dilemmas of Identity in Contemporary Life*, New York: Basic Books.

Giddens, Anthony 1984, *The Constitution of Society*, Cambridge: Polity Press.

1985, *The Nation State and Violence*, Berkeley: University of California Press.

1990, *The Consequences of Modernity*, Cambridge: Polity Press.

1991, *Modernity and Self-Identity: Self and Society in the Late Modern Age*, Cambridge: Polity Press.

1992, *The Transformation of Intimacy*, Cambridge: Polity Press.

Gillett, Grant 1994, 'Beyond the Orthodox: Heresy in Medicine and Social Science', *Social Science and Medicine*, 39, 9: 1125–31.

Gilligan, Carol 1982, *In a Different Voice*, Cambridge MA: Harvard University Press.

Gilligan, Carol, Ward, Janie V. and Taylor, Jill M. 1988, *Mapping the Moral Domain: A Contribution of Women's Thinking to Psychological Theory and Education*, Cambridge MA: Harvard University Press.

Gilman, Sander L. 1988, *Disease and Representation: Images of Illness from Madness to Aids*, Ithaca: Cornell University Press.

Gilroy, Paul 1987, *There Ain't No Black in the Union Jack*, London: Hutchinson.

1993a, *Small Acts*, London: Serpent's Tail.

1993b, *The Black Atlantic*, Cambridge MA: Harvard University Press.

Goldfarb, Jeffrey C. 1991, *The Cynical Society*, Chicago: University of Chicago Press.

Grathoff, Richard H. 1970, *The Structure of Social Inconsistencies: A Contribution to a Unified Theory of Play, Game and Social Action*, The Hague: Nijhoff.

Greenfield, Liah 1992, *Nationalism: Five Roads to Modernity*, Cambridge MA: Harvard University Press.

Gregory, Derek and Urry, John (eds.) 1985, *Social Relations and Spatial Structures*, London: Macmillan.

Habermas, Jurgen 1984, *The Theory of Communicative Action: Vol. I: Reason and Rationalization of Society*, Cambridge: Polity Press.

1987, *The Theory of Communicative Action: Vol. II: The Critique of Functionalist Reason*, Cambridge: Polity Press.

1989, *The Structural Transformation of the Public Sphere*, Cambridge: Polity Press.

1990, *The Philosophical Discourse of Modernity*, Cambridge: Polity Press.

Halbwachs, Maurice 1975, *Les cadres sociaux de la mémoire*, Paris: Mouton (original edition 1925).

Hall, Stephen, Keeter, Larry and Williamson, Jennifer 1993, 'Toward an Understanding of Humor as Popular Culture in American Society', *Journal of American Culture*, 16, 2: 1–6.

Hall, Stuart and Jacques, Martin (eds.) 1989, *New Times: The Changing Face of Politics in the 1990s*, London: Lawrence and Wishart.

Hall, Stuart and Jefferson, Tony (eds.) 1979, *Resistance Through Rituals: Youth Subcultures in Post-war Britain*, London: Macmillan.

Hanson, Shirley M. and Bozett, Frederick W. 1985, *Dimensions of Fatherhood*, London: Sage.

Harré, Rom and Gillett, Grant 1994, *The Discoursive Mind*, London: Sage.

Harvey, David 1989, *The Condition of Post-Modernity*, Oxford: Blackwell.

Hassard, John (ed.) 1990, *The Sociology of Time*, London: Macmillan.

Haug, Frigga (ed.) 1987, *Female Sexualization*, London: Verso.

Hebdige, Dick 1979, *Subcultures: The Meaning of Style*, London: Methuen.
  1988, *Hiding in the Light: On Images and Things*, London: Routledge.

Hinde, Robert A. 1987, *Individuals, Relationships and Culture*, Cambridge: Cambridge University Press.

Hirsch, Eli 1982, *The Concept of Identity*, Oxford: Oxford University Press.

Hobson, J. Allan 1988, *The Dreaming Brain*, New York: Basic Books.

Hugues, Robert 1993, *Culture of Complaint: The Fraying of America*, Oxford: Oxford University Press.

Humphrey, Nicholas 1992, *A History of Mind*, New York: Simon and Schuster.

Huyssen, Andreas 1986, *After the Great Divide: Modernism, Mass Culture, Postmodernism*, London: Macmillan.

Isaac, Rael Jean and Armat, Virginia C. 1990, *Madness in the Streets: How Psychiatry Abandoned the Mentally Ill*, New York: Free Press.

Jacobus, Mary, Keller, Evelyn Fox and Shuttleworth, Sally (eds.) 1990, *Body/Politics: Women and the Discourses of Science*, London: Routledge.

Jameson, Fredric 1991, *Postmodernism, or the Cultural Logic of Late Capitalism*, London: Verso.

Jardine, Alice A. 1985, *Gynesis*, New York: Cornell University Press.

Joas, Hans 1992, *Das Kreativitat des Handels*, Frankfurt: Suhrkamp.

Johnson, Leslie 1993, *The Modern Girl: Girlhood and Growing Up*, Buckingham: Open University Press.

Johnson, Mark 1987, *The Body in the Mind: The Bodily Basis of Meaning, Imagination and Reason*, Chicago: University of Chicago Press.

Johnston, Hank and Klandermans, Bert (eds.) 1995, *Social Movements and Culture*, Minneapolis: University of Minnesota Press.

Kearl, Michael C. 1989, *Endings: A Sociology of Death and Dying*, Oxford University Press.

Keen, Sam 1991, *Fire in the Belly. On Being a Man*, New York: Bantam Books.

Kepel, Gilles 1987, *Les Banlieues de l'Islam*, Paris: Seuil.
  1994, *A' l'Ouest d'Allah*, Paris: Seuil.

Klivingston, Kenneth (ed.) 1993, *The Science of Mind*, Cambridge MA: MIT Press.

Kosslyn, Stephen and Andersen, Richard (eds.) 1992, *Frontiers in Cognitive Neuroscience*, Cambridge MA: MIT Press.

Kristeva, Julia 1989, *Black Sun: Depression and Melancholia*, New York: Columbia University Press.

Laidi, Zaki 1994, *Un monde privé de sens*, Paris: Fayard.

Lalive d'Epinay, Christian 1983, 'La vie quotidienne. Essai de construction d'un concept sociologique et anthropologique', *Cahiers Intérnationaux de Sociologie*, 74: 13–38.

Lamb, Michael E. 1987, *The Father's Role*, Hillsdale: Erlbaum.

Lamont, Michelle and Fournier, Marcel 1992, *Cultivating Differences: Symbolic Boundaries and the Making of Inequalities*, Chicago: University of Chicago Press.

Landes, David S. 1984, *Revolution in Time: Clocks and the Making of the Modern World*, Cambridge MA: Harvard University Press 1984.

Larana, Enrique, Johnston, Hank and Gusfield, Joseph R. (eds.) 1994, *New Social Movements: From Ideology to Identity*, Philadelphia: Temple University Press.

Lasch, Christopher 1978, *The Culture of Narcissism*, New York: Norton.

1984, *The Minimal Self*, London: Pan Books.

Lash, Scott and Friedman, Jonathan (eds.) 1992, *Modernity and Identity*, Oxford, Blackwell.

Lash, Scott and Urry, John 1987, *The End of Organized Capitalism*, Cambridge: Polity Press.

Latour, Bruno 1987, *Science in Action*, Milton Keynes: Open University Press.

Laughlin, Charles D., McManus, John and D'Aquili, Eugene G. 1990, *Brain, Symbol and Experience: Toward a Neurophenomenology of Human Consciousness*, Boston: New Science Library.

Lefebvre, Henri 1991, *The Production of Space*, Oxford: Blackwell.

Levin, David M. and Salomon, George F. (1990) 'The Discoursive Formation of the Body in the History of Medicine', *Journal of Medicine and Philosophy*, 15, 5: 515–37.

Levinson, Daniel 1978, *The Seasons of a Man's Life*, New York: Knopf.

Little, W. Kenneth 1991, 'The Rhetoric of Romance and the Simulation of Tradition in Circus Clown Performance', *Semiotica* 85, 3–4: 227–55.

1993, 'Masochism, Spectacle, and the 'Broken Mirror' Clown Entree: A Note on the Anthropology of Performance in Postmodern Culture', *Cultural Anthropology*, 8, 1: 117–29.

Locke, Don C. 1992, *Increasing Multicultural Understanding*, London: Sage.

Lombardo, William K., Cretser, Gary A., Lombardo, Barbara and Mathis, Sharon L. 1983, 'For Cryin' Out Loud There Is a Sex Difference', *Sex-Roles*, 9, 9: 987–95.

Lorber, Judith 1994, *Paradoxes of Gender*, New Haven CT: Yale University Press.

Luard, Evan 1990, *The Globalization of Politics: The Changed Focus of Political Action in the Modern World*, London: Macmillan.

Luhmann, Niklas 1987, 'The Future Cannot Begin: Temporal Structures in Modern Society', *Social Research*, 53: 130-52.

Lundell, Torborg 1993, 'An Experiential Exploration of Why Men and Women Laugh', *Humor*, 6, 3: 299–317.

Lupton, Deborah 1994, *Medicine as Culture: Illness, Disease and the Body in Western Societies,* London: Sage.

Luske, Bruce 1990, *Mirrors of Madness: Patrolling the Psychic Border*, New York: Aldine

McGhee, Paul E. and Chapman, Anthony J. (eds.) 1980, *Children's Humor*, Chichester: Wiley.

McGhee, Paul E. and Goldstein Jeffrey H. (eds.) 1983, *Handbook of Humor Research*, New York: Springer Verlag.

McGrath, Joseph E. 1988, *The Social Psychology of Time*, Newbury Park: Sage.

McGrath, Joseph E. and Kelly Janice R. 1986, *Time and Human Interaction: Towards a Social Psychology of Time*, New York: Guilford Press.

McGrew, Anthony G. and Lewis, Paul G. (eds.) 1992, *Global Politics. Globalization and the Nation State*, Cambridge: Polity Press.

McNamee, Sheila and Gergen, Kenneth J. 1992, *Therapy as Social Construction*, London: Sage.

McQuail, Davis 1992, *Media Performance*, London: Sage.

Maffesoli, Michel 1995, *The Time of the Tribes*, London: Sage.

Maheu, Louis (ed.) 1995, *Social Movements and Social Classes: The Future of Collective Action*, London: Sage.

Margolis, Howard 1993, *Paradigms and Barriers: How Habits of Mind Govern Scientific Beliefs*, University of Chicago Press.

Maturana, Humberto and Varela, Francisco 1980, *Autopoiesis and Cognition*, Boston: Reidel.

Melucci, Alberto 1989, *Nomads of the Present*, Philadelphia: Temple University Press.

  1996, *Challenging Codes: Collective Action in The Information Age*, Cambridge: Cambridge University Press.

Middleton, David and Edwards, Derek (eds.) 1990, *Collective Remembering*, London: Sage.

Middleton, Richard 1990, *Studying Popular Music*, Milton Keynes: Open University Press.

Mindell, Arnold 1985, *River's Way: The Process Science of the Dreambody*, London: Routledge and Kegan Paul.

Mitterauer, Michael 1992, *A History of Youth*, Oxford: Blackwell.

Modleski, Tania (ed.) 1986, *Studies in Entertainment: Critical Approaches to Mass Culture*, Bloomington IN: Indiana University Press.

  1982, *Loving with a Vengeance: Mass-produced Fantasies for Women*, Hamden: Archon Books.

  1991, *Feminism Without Women: Culture and Criticism in a 'Post-feminist' Age*, Hamden: Archon Books.

Momeyer, Richard W. 1988, *Confronting Death*, Bloomington IN: Indiana University Press.

Morin Edgar 1980, *La méthode: 2. La vie de la vie*, Paris: Seuil.

1986, *La méthode: 3. La connaissance de la connaissance*, Paris: Seuil.

Morley, David 1992, *Television: Audiences and Cultural Studies*, London: Routledge.

Morris, Aldon D. and Mueller, Carol McClurg (eds.) 1992, *Frontiers in Social Movement Theory*, New Haven: Yale University Press.

Mukerji, Chandra and Schudson, Michael (eds.) 1991, *Rethinking Popular Culture: Contemporary Perspectives in Cultural Studies*, Berkeley: University of California Press.

Murphy, Michael 1992, *The Future of the Body*, Los Angeles: Tarcher.

Namer, Gérard 1987, *Mémoire et société*, Paris: Méridiens Klincksieck.

Nava, Mica 1992, *Changing Cultures: Feminism, Youth and Consumerism*, London: Sage.

Norman Donald A. 1988, *The Psychology of Everyday Things*, New York: Basic Books.

Novotny, Helga 1992, 'Time and Social Theory. Towards a Social Theory of Time', *Time and Society* 1: 421–54.

O'Neil, John 1989, *The Communicative Body*, Evanston: Northwestern University Press.

Oakley, David A. 1985, *Brain and the Mind*, London: Methuen.

Ornstein, Michael 1992, 'Aspects of the Political and Personal Sociology of AIDS: Knowledge, Policy Attitudes and Risks', *Canadian Review of Sociology and Anthropology*, 29, 3: 243–65.

Ornstein, Robert E. and Sobel, David S. 1987, *The Healing Brain*, New York: Simon and Schuster.

Oring, Elliot 1992, *Jokes and their Relations*, Lexington: University Press of Kentucky.

Parfit, Derek 1984, *Reasons and Persons*, Cambridge: Cambridge University Press.

Peat, F. David 1987, *Synchronicity: The Bridge between Matter and Mind*, New York: Bantam Books.

Pessoa, Fernando 1991, *The Book of Disquietude*, Manchester: Carcanet.

Pizzorno, Alessandro 1993, 'All You Can Do with Reasons', *International Studies in the Philosophy of Science*, 7, 1: 75–80.

Plessner, Helmuth 1970, *Laughing and Crying: A Study of the Limits of Human Behavior*, Evanston: Northwestern University Press.

Porteous, Janice 1989, 'Humor and Social Life', *Philosophy East and West*, 39, 3: 279–88.

Pratt, Michael W. and Norris, Joan E. 1994, *The Social Psychology of Aging*, Oxford: Blackwell.

Prior, Lindsay 1989, *The Social Organisation of Death: Medical Discourse and Social Practices in Belfast*, London: Macmillan.

Purce, Jill 1974, *The Mystic Spiral*, London: Thames and Hudson.

Ricoeur, Paul 1974, *The Conflict of Interpretations: Essays in Hermeneutics*, Evanston: Northwestern University Press.

1976, *Interpretation Theory: Discourse and the Surplus of Meaning*, Fort Worth: Texas Christian University Press.

1984, *Time and Narrative*, Chicago: University of Chicago Press.

Robertson, Roland 1992, *Globalization: Social Theory and Global Culture*, London: Sage.

Robinson, Bryan E. and Barret, Robert L. 1986, *The Developing Father*, New York: Guilford Press.

Root-Bernstein, Robert 1989, *Discovering*, Cambridge MA: Harvard University Press.

Rorty, Richard 1989, *Contingency, Irony and Solidarity*, Cambridge: Cambridge University Press.

Rose, Margaret A. 1991, *The Post-Modern and the Post-Industrial*, Cambridge: Cambridge University Press.

Roszak, Theodore 1992, *The Voice of the Earth*, New York: Simon and Schuster.

Runco, Mark A. and Albert, Robert S. (eds.) 1990, *Theories of Creativity*, Newbury Park: Sage.

Salmon, Charles T. (ed.) 1989, *Information Campaigns*, London: Sage.

Salmon, J. Warren (ed.) 1984, *Alternative Medicine: Popular and Policy Perspectives*, London: Tavistock.

Schank, Roger C. and Abelson, Robert 1977, *Scripts, Plans, Goals and Understanding*, Hillsdale: Erlbaum.

Schlesinger, Philip 1991, *Media, State and Nation*, London: Sage.

Scull, Andrew 1993, *The Most Solitary of Afflictions: Madness and Society in Britain 1700-1900*, New Haven: Yale University Press.

Seidman, Steven and Wagner, David G. 1992, *Postmodernism and Social Theory*, Oxford: Blackwell.

Sennett, Richard 1993, *The Conscience of the Eye: The Design and Social Life of Cities*, London: Faber.

Sharma, Ursula 1993, 'Contextualizing Alternative Medicine: The Exotic, the Marginal and the Perfectly Mundane', *Anthropology Today*, 9, 4: 15–18.

Shaver, Phillip R. (ed.) 1985, *Self, Situations and Social Behavior*, London: Sage.

Shelton, Beth Anne 1992, *Women, Men and Time*, Westport CN: Greenwood Press.

Shields, Rod (ed.) 1992, *Lifestyle Shopping: The Subjects of Consumption*, London: Routledge.

Shilling, Chris 1993, *The Body and Social Theory*, London: Sage.

Shils, Edward 1981, *Tradition*, London: Faber and Faber.

Shotter, John 1993, *Conversational Realities: Constructing Life through Language*, London: Sage.

Shotter, John 1993, *Cultural Politics of Everyday Life*, Toronto: University of Toronto Press.

Shotter, John and Gergen, Kenneth J. (eds.) 1989, *Texts of Identity*, London: Sage.

Shorter, Edward 1992, *From Paralysis to Fatigue: A History of Psychosomatic Illness in the Modern Era*, New York: Free Press.

Siegel, Lee 1987, *Laughing Matters: Comic Tradition in India*, Chicago: University of Chicago Press.

Sirianni, Carmen 1988, *Work, Time and Inequality*, Oxford: Oxford University Press.

Smart, Barry 1992, *Modern Conditions, Postmodern Controversies*, London: Routledge.

Smith, Dorothy 1988, *The Everyday World as Problematic: A Feminist Sociology*, Milton Keynes: Open University Press.

Smith, Hedrick 1992, *The Media and the Gulf War*, Washington: Seven Locks Press.

Snyder, Salomon 1989, *Brainstorming*, Cambridge MA: Harvard University Press.

Spivak, Gayatri C. 1987, *In Other Worlds*, London: Methuen.

Starobinski, Jean 1983, *Portrait de l'artiste en Saltimbanque*, Paris: Flammarion.

Stebbins, Robert A. 1990, *The Laugh-Makers*, Montreal: McGill University Press.

Sternberg, Robert J. (ed.) 1988, *The Nature of Creativity*, Cambridge: Cambridge University Press.

Suls, Jerry (ed.) 1993, *The Self in Social Perspective*, Hillsdale: Erlbaum.

Tarrow, Sidney 1994, *Power in Movement: Social Movements Collective Action and Politics*, Cambridge: Cambridge University Press.

Taussig, Michael 1993, *Mimesis and Alterity: A Particular History of the Senses*, London: Routledge.

Taylor, Charles 1989, *Sources of the Self: The Making of the Modern Identity*, Cambridge MA: Harvard University Press.

1992, *Ethics of Authenticity*, Cambridge MA: Harvard University Press.

1992, *Multiculturalism and 'The Politics of Recognition'*, Princeton: Princeton University Press.

Thetard, Henry 1978, *La merveilleuse histoire du cirque*, Paris: Julliard.

Thorson, James A. 1995, *Aging in a Changing Society*, Belmont: Wadsworth.

Tomlison, Alan (ed.) 1990, *Consumption, Identity and Style: Marketing, Meanings and the Packaging of Leisure*, London: Routledge.

Toulmin, Stephen E. 1990, *Cosmopolis: The Hidden Agenda of Modernity*, New York: Free Press.

Touraine, Alain 1984, *Le Retour de l'Acteur*, Paris: Fayard.

Touraine, Alain 1994, *Critique of Modernity*, Oxford: Blackwell.

Turner, Bryan S. (ed.) 1990, *Theories of Modernity and Postmodernity*, London: Sage.

Turner, Bryan S. 1992, *Regulating Bodies. Essays in Medical Sociology*, London: Sage.

Turner, Victor 1982, *From Ritual to Theatre*, New York: Performing Arts Journal Publications.

Vincent, Jean-Didier 1986, *Biologie des passions*, Paris: Odile Jacob.

Von Franz, Marie-Louise 1978, *Time, Rhythm and Repose*, London: Thames and Hudson.

Walzer, Michael 1992 (1977), *Just and Unjust Wars*, New York: Basic Books.

Wardwell, Walter I. 1994, 'Alternative Medicine in the United States', *Social Science and Medicine*, 38, 8: 1061–1068.

Watney, Simon 1987, *Policing Desire: Pornography, Aids and the Media*, London: Comedia.

Watzlawick, Paul (ed) 1984, *The Invented Reality*, London: Norton.

Weisberg, Robert W. 1986, *Creativity and Other Myths*, New York: W.H. Freeman.

White, Harrison C. 1992, *Identity and Control: A Structural Theory of Social Action*, Princeton: Princeton University Press.

White, Harrison C. 1993, *Careers and Creativity*, Boulder: Westview Press.

Willis, Paul 1990, *Common Culture*, Boulder: Westview Press.

Willis, Paul 1990, *Common Culture: Symbolic Work at Play in the Everyday Cultures of the Young*, Milton Keynes: Open University Press.

Winfree, Arthur T. 1987, *The Timing of Biological Clocks*, New York: Scientific American.

Wolpe, Paul Root 1994, 'The Dynamics of Heresy in Profession', *Social Science and Medicine*, 39, 9: 1133–1148.

Wolton, Dominique 1991, *Wargames: L'information et la guerre*, Paris: Flammarion.

Woolley, Benjamin 1992, *Virtual Worlds*, London: Penguin.

Wuthnow, Robert 1987, *Meaning and Moral Order*, Berkeley: University of California Press.

Yiannis, Gabriel and Lang, Tim 1995, *The Unmanageable Consumer: Contemporary Consumption and its Fragmentations*, London; Sage.

Young, Michael D. 1988, *The Metronomic Society*, Cambridge MA: Harvard University Press.

Zerubavel, Eviatar 1981, *Hidden Rythms*, Chicago: University of Chicago Press.

Zerubavel, Eviatar 1985, *The Seven-Day Circle*, New York: Free Press.

Ziehe, Thomas 1991, *Zeitvergleiche: Jugend in Kulturelle Modernisierung*, Munich: Juventa

Zolberg, Vera 1990, *Constructing a Sociology of the Arts*, Cambridge: Cambridge University Press.

Index